T0109589

HOW TO CARE ABOUT ANIMALS

ANCIENT WISDOM FOR MODERN READERS

■ ■ ■ ■

For a full list of titles in the series, go to https://press.princeton.edu
/series/ancient-wisdom-for-modern-readers.

HOW TO CARE
ABOUT ANIMALS

An Ancient Guide
to Creatures Great and Small

Porphyry and Friends

Selected, translated, and introduced
by M. D. Usher

PRINCETON UNIVERSITY PRESS

PRINCETON AND OXFORD

Published by Princeton University Press
41 William Street, Princeton, New Jersey 08540
6 Oxford Street, Woodstock, Oxfordshire OX20 1TR

press.princeton.edu

All Rights Reserved

ISBN 9780691240435
ISBN (e-book) 9780691240442

British Library Cataloging-in-Publication Data is available

Editorial: Rob Tempio and Chloe Coy
Production Editorial: Sara Lerner
Text Design: Pamela L. Schnitter
Jacket Design: Heather Hansen
Production: Erin Suydam
Publicity: Tyler Hubbert and Carmen Jimenez
Copyeditor: Kathleen Kageff

Jacket Credit: Marble grave stele of a little girl, courtesy of The Metropolitan Museum of Art

This book has been composed in Stempel Garamond

Printed on acid-free paper. ∞

Printed in the United States of America

1 3 5 7 9 10 8 6 4 2

CONTENTS

ACKNOWLEDGMENTS

This book was conceived and brought to parturition during a fellowship at the Institute for Advanced Study at Aix-Marseille University (Fondation IMéRA) in 2021–22. I would like to thank colleagues and friends at IMéRA and the French Network of Institutes for Advanced Study (RFIEA/FIAS) for that residency, which was funded by a Marie Skłodowska-Curie international mobility award.[1] I'm indebted as well to the University of Vermont for granting a research leave that made it possible for me to accept the fellowship. Special thanks, too, to students in my Honors College seminar on this topic, who kindly beta tested the book with me during the fall 2022 semester: Cassie Beeler, Abby Bell, Anya Doughertry, Julia Gamache, Madeline Harreld, Isabel Homsi, Camille Howard, Veronica Julian, Leda Kahn, Katarina Lile, Jacob Mccoy, Kegan Muhiudeen, Jonas O'Mara, Sam Pernia, Sebastian Redondo, Maclan Roberts, Bri Seawick, Jenna Siders, Olivia Tibbetts, Jaden Trask, and Petra Waterstreet.

INTRODUCTION

Animals are all the rage these days. As human creatures become increasingly concerned about the precariousness of life on an overheated, over-crowded planet, a new fascination with the resil-ience, agency, and nobility of nonhuman creatures has recaptured our collective imaginations, not unlike how these same qualities transfixed our Paleolithic forebears, the cave painters of Africa, Europe, and Australia, over thirty-thousand years ago. A book about animals thus needs no justifi-cation. But what about a book about ancient Greek and Roman thinking about animals?

The Greeks and Romans, amid all their mag-nificent cultural achievements and reckless, de-structive behavior, nonetheless lived closer than most of us to the sources of their survival. This afforded them a sensitivity to their environs and fellow creatures, born of necessity, that can help disabuse us of our shortsighted presentism and

counteract our technology-enhanced disconnect-
edness from Nature. It is astounding how rele-
vant the ancients still are in this regard. Not many
contemporary readers will know, for example,
about the compelling arguments Porphyry makes
for vegetarianism (selection no. 12), long before a
plant-based diet started garnering headlines. Plutarch's seriocomic exposition of the rationality
and inherent dignity of animals—put on the lips
of one of Circe's pigs (selection no. 11)—is so fresh
that it sounds like it was written just yesterday.
The knowledge the poet Theognis derived from
Greek sponge divers about the behavior of octo-
pods (selection no. 3) puts the awe engendered by
the Netflix hit *My Octopus Teacher* (2021) into
new perspective over the *longue durée*. Aristotle's
exordium to the scientific study of animal mor-
phology and behavior (selection no. 1) remains
unparalleled for its elegance and insight. Seneca
argues that human beings are morally and ecologically inferior to other animals (selection no. 6),
presenting us thereby with a parable for the An-
thropocene that indicts global consumption and
depletion of habitats and natural resources. *How
to Care about Animals* attempts to capture and
leverage the zeitgeist on these issues.

Of course, the ancients were far from perfect in their treatment of animals. The elder Pliny's account of elephant abuse by Romans and Carthaginians (selection no. 10) is both heartbreaking and infuriating. Interspecies interaction is always fraught with peril, as the myth of Cyparissus (selection no. 9), the fate of Tiberius's raven (selection no. 8), and Aesop's fable of the Old Ox and Young Steer (selection no. 2) make all too plain. I have experienced this peril myself on our farm, where it's impossible to avoid run-ins with both domesticated animals (sheep, cows, donkeys, chickens, dogs, goats, pigs) and other critters (deer, mice, squirrels, rabbits, coyotes, racoons, fisher cats, opossums, bears). A runaway goat or pig, for example, destroys your garden. A bear mauls your beehive. Deer ruin your specimen evergreens. Squirrels devour the birdseed you set out for your feathered friends in winter. The fisher cat beheads your chickens. Carpenter bees bore holes in the siding of your house. Coyotes rip your lambs to shreds. Animals can't help themselves: they do what Nature has designed them to do, or what we train them to do (which, incidentally, reveals an impressive latent capability in their natural competences). We humans, however, have the capacity

for choice and can exercise it in ways that other animals cannot. When it comes to interacting with them, that puts the moral burden on us.

People with little actual experience with animals sometimes decry Man's supposed dominance over them. I have two comments about that. First, in surveying what I find to be some of the most compelling contemporary writing about animals, I'm struck by how many of our most important thinkers are women—Jenny Diski, Temple Grandin, Donna Haraway, Christine Korsgaard, Vicki Hearne.[1] In *Adam's Task: Calling Animals by Name*, Hearne, a professional dog trainer with a philosophical bent, describes how she broke her pointer Salty from the habit of digging holes in the backyard. When it comes to discouraging undesirable behavior, Hearne believed that dogs respond best to the kind of negative reinforcement and correction that they would encounter in their natural state as members of a pack. So, she would join Salty on the back lawn, and they would dig a hole together as if it were a game, whereupon Hearne would fill the hole with water, and then dunk Salty's head in it. A few holes later and Salty was cured. Quick to anticipate

criticism of her technique, Hearne insists that *"this has nothing to do with either punishment or authority, and if it is corrupted by either then it becomes cruel."*[2]

Which brings me to my second point. Whether one agrees with Hearne's methods or not, what the Salty episode illustrates is that our interactions with animals are, and must always be, relational, not merely transactional.[3] (Salty has a name, and her agency is acknowledged; to help her flourish in her adopted human environment, Hearne applies "tough love" to break her of a destructive habit that is unacceptable to the pack ethos.) In my experience, a relational approach to animals involves cooperation and mutual respect, not dominance. Believe me, there is no way you're going to get a donkey to go through a gate it doesn't want to go through. You need to convince it, make it think that going through the gate was its own idea. Likewise, a Scottish Highland bull is not to be trifled with. You can't just push him where you want him to go. You must incentivize him.

In dealing with animals, you ultimately learn a lot about yourself and your own limitations.

In fact, historically speaking, our interactions with fellow creatures are best described as a long process of *codomestication*.[4] The same is true philosophically, too. To adapt a phrase from Temple Grandin, which is adumbrated by Porphyry in the treatise excerpted as selection no. 12, how we treat animals can make us better human beings. Even dangerous, predatory animals can improve us. Werner Herzog's film about the grisly death of bear conservationist Timothy Treadwell (*Grizzly Man*, 2005) provides a stark and necessary warning about crossing the line with wild animals. Yet anthropologist Nastassja Martin, who was maimed and disfigured by a bear while doing fieldwork in Russia's Kamchatka Peninsula in 2015, managed to turn her harrowing experience into a powerful meditation on interspecies *affinities*.[5]

The selections from Greek and Roman writers included here likewise run the gamut of human responses to living on a planet cohabited by other animals. Those responses range from scientific curiosity, emotional attachment, and religious awe to self-interested neglect, unthinking disregard, and calculated exploitation. *How to Care*

about Animals, then, in claiming to be a guide to creatures great and small, inevitably reflects an ongoing, evolutionary process in which our own species is still entangled.

So let us take auguries, for which William Blake's "Auguries of Innocence" (1803) provides the rawest material. Blake's poem consists of a series of scenarios, expressed in rhyming couplets, wherein human wrongdoing portends some larger existential doom. Most apt for our purposes here are the warnings attached to the mistreatment of Nature's nonhuman agents. Blake almost casts our relationship to our fellow creatures as one of Newton's Universal Laws: For every action, it is implied, there is an equal and opposite reaction. Given the fragility of prevailing conditions, it would behoove us all to err on the side of caution:

> A Robin Red breast in a Cage
> Puts all Heaven in a Rage
>
> A dog starvd at his Masters Gate
> Predicts the ruin of the State

HOW TO CARE ABOUT ANIMALS

Each outcry of the hunted Hare
A fibre from the Brain does tear

He who shall hurt the little Wren
Shall never be belovd by Men

Kill not the Moth nor Butterfly
For the Last Judgment draweth nigh

HOW TO CARE ABOUT ANIMALS

1. Small Is Beautiful (Aristotle, *Parts of Animals* 1.5)

In 1980, art critic John Berger published a widely read and highly influential essay entitled "Why Look at Animals?" about the alienation that sets in between human and nonhuman animal species in a capitalistic age of mechanical reproduction. Why look at animals? The following excerpt is Aristotle's answer to that question, formulated over two thousand years prior. Somehow, in only a few paragraphs, Aristotle manages to present the best case perhaps ever made for the inherent worth of both physical and metaphysical pursuits. Remarkably fresh and contemporary is his insistence that all scientific investigation, of whatever sort, should be concerned with systemic wholes, about which, he says, looking at animals has much to teach us.

Τῶν οὐσιῶν ὅσαι φύσει συνεστᾶσι, τὰς μὲν <λέ-
γομεν> ἀγενήτους καὶ ἀφθάρτους εἶναι τὸν ἅπαντα
αἰῶνα, τὰς δὲ μετέχειν γενέσεως καὶ φθορᾶς. συμ-
βέβηκε δὲ περὶ μὲν ἐκείνας τιμίας οὔσας καὶ θείας
ἐλάττους ἡμῖν ὑπάρχειν θεωρίας (καὶ γὰρ ἐξ ὧν ἄν
τις σκέψαιτο περὶ αὐτῶν, καὶ περὶ ὧν εἰδέναι πο-
θοῦμεν, παντελῶς ἐστιν ὀλίγα τὰ φανερὰ κατὰ τὴν
αἴσθησιν), περὶ δὲ τῶν φθαρτῶν φυτῶν τε καὶ ζῴων
εὐποροῦμεν μᾶλλον πρὸς τὴν γνῶσιν διὰ τὸ σύ-
ντροφον· πολλὰ γὰρ περὶ ἕκαστον γένος λάβοι τις
ἂν τῶν ὑπαρχόντων βουλόμενος διαπονεῖν ἱκανῶς.
ἔχει δ᾽ ἑκάτερα χάριν.

τῶν μὲν γὰρ εἰ καὶ κατὰ μικρὸν ἐφαπτόμεθα,
ὅμως διὰ τὴν τιμιότητα τοῦ γνωρίζειν ἥδιον ἢ τὰ
παρ᾽ ἡμῖν ἅπαντα, ὥσπερ καὶ τῶν ἐρωμένων τὸ
τυχὸν καὶ μικρὸν μόριον κατιδεῖν ἥδιόν ἐστιν ἢ
πολλὰ ἕτερα καὶ μεγάλα δι᾽ ἀκριβείας ἰδεῖν· τὰ δὲ
διὰ τὸ μᾶλλον καὶ πλείω γνωρίζειν αὐτῶν λαμβάνει τὴν τῆς ἐπιστήμης ὑπεροχήν, ἔτι δὲ διὰ τὸ πλη-
σιαίτερα ἡμῶν εἶναι καὶ τῆς φύσεως οἰκειότερα
ἀντικαταλλάττεταί τι πρὸς τὴν περὶ τὰ θεῖα
φιλοσοφίαν.

We assert that there two sorts of beings in Nature, those that are without origin, eternal, and indestructible, and those that participate in processes of birth and decay. It follows that those beings in the first category, although precious because divine, are less susceptible to investigation because there is scant empirical evidence for what we yearn to know about them. But concerning beings that perish, like plants and animals, we are better provided for in gaining knowledge because we live alongside them. Indeed, anyone who cares enough to put in the work can discover a great deal about each of their various kinds. Nonetheless, both sorts of beings have their own charm.

So, while it's clear that our grasp of eternal subjects is slight, nonetheless, because they are precious, knowledge of them is more delightful than knowledge of everything else that falls in our orbit, just as it is more delightful to get a partial, fleeting glimpse of those we love than to review a host of quotidian details with precision, even if those, too, are important. Subjects of study on Earth, on the other hand, because we have more and better information about them, take priority

ἐπεὶ δὲ περὶ ἐκείνων διήλθομεν λέγοντες τὸ φαινόμενον ἡμῖν, λοιπὸν περὶ τῆς ζωικῆς φύσεως εἰπεῖν, μηδὲν παραλιπόντας εἰς δύναμιν μήτε ἀτιμότερον μήτε τιμιώτερον. καὶ γὰρ ἐν τοῖς μὴ κεχαρισμένοις αὐτῶν πρὸς τὴν αἴσθησιν κατὰ τὴν θεωρίαν ὅμως ἡ δημιουργήσασα φύσις ἀμηχάνους ἡδονὰς παρέχει τοῖς δυναμένοις τὰς αἰτίας γνωρίζειν καὶ φύσει φιλοσόφοις.

καὶ γὰρ ἂν εἴη παράλογον καὶ ἄτοπον, εἰ τὰς μὲν εἰκόνας αὐτῶν θεωροῦντες χαίρομεν ὅτι τὴν δημιουργήσασαν τέχνην συνθεωροῦμεν, οἷον τὴν γραφικὴν ἢ τὴν πλαστικήν, αὐτῶν δὲ τῶν φύσει συνεστώτων μὴ μᾶλλον ἀγαπῷμεν τὴν θεωρίαν, δυνάμενοί γε τὰς αἰτίας καθορᾶν. διὸ δεῖ μὴ δυσχεραίνειν παιδικῶς τὴν περὶ τῶν ἀτιμοτέρων ζῴων ἐπίσκεψιν· ἐν πᾶσι γὰρ τοῖς φυσικοῖς ἔνεστί τι θαυμαστόν·

when it comes to knowledge because they are nearer to us and their nature more akin to our nature. Such pursuits compensate somewhat for the philosophy that concerns itself with theology.

So, now that we have rehearsed and presented our views on theological subjects, it remains to speak about animals and their nature. To the extent that we can, we will leave no animal out, whether it be regarded as valueless or highly prized. For even in dealing with animals that are less pleasing to the senses, when a person of natural philosophic bent considers them from a scientific point of view, someone who can understand the causes of things, Nature, in displaying its handiwork, presents pleasures beyond compare.

It would be strange and illogical, I would add, to take pleasure in looking at artistic representations of animals, and to study the craftmanship that produced them, say, in painting or sculpture, but not to welcome even more so studying the actual creatures fashioned by Nature, especially when we can understand the causes from which they're sprung. Therefore, we must not flinch, as if we were children, at the careful consideration of less-esteemed animals, for in all of Nature there is something wonderful.

καὶ καθάπερ Ἡράκλειτος λέγεται πρὸς τοὺς ξέ-
νους εἰπεῖν τοὺς βουλομένους ἐντυχεῖν αὐτῷ, οἳ
ἐπειδὴ προσιόντες εἶδον αὐτὸν θερόμενον πρὸς τῷ
ἰπνῷ ἔστησαν (ἐκέλευε γὰρ αὐτοὺς εἰσιέναι θαρ-
ροῦντας· εἶναι γὰρ καὶ ἐνταῦθα θεούς), οὕτω καὶ
πρὸς τὴν ζήτησιν περὶ ἑκάστου τῶν ζῴων προσιέ-
ναι δεῖ μὴ δυσωπούμενον, ὡς ἐν ἅπασιν ὄντος τινὸς
φυσικοῦ καὶ καλοῦ. Τὸ γὰρ μὴ τυχόντως ἀλλ᾽ ἕνεκά
τινος ἐν τοῖς τῆς φύσεως ἔργοις ἐστὶ καὶ μάλιστα·
οὗ δ᾽ ἕνεκα συνέστηκεν ἢ γέγονε τέλους, τὴν τοῦ
καλοῦ χώραν εἴληφεν.

εἰ δέ τις τὴν περὶ τῶν ἄλλων ζῴων θεωρίαν ἄτιμον εἶναι νενόμικε, τὸν αὐτὸν τρόπον οἴεσθαι χρὴ
καὶ περὶ αὑτοῦ· οὐκ ἔστι γὰρ ἄνευ πολλῆς δυσχε-
ρείας ἰδεῖν ἐξ ὧν συνέστηκε τὸ τῶν ἀνθρώπων
γένος, οἷον αἷμα, σάρκες, ὀστᾶ, φλέβες καὶ τὰ
τοιαῦτα μόρια. ὁμοίως τε δεῖ νομίζειν τὸν περὶ οὑτι-
νοσοῦν τῶν μορίων ἢ τῶν σκευῶν διαλεγόμενον
μὴ περὶ τῆς ὕλης ποιεῖσθαι τὴν μνήμην, μηδὲ ταύτης
χάριν, ἀλλὰ τῆς ὅλης μορφῆς, οἷον καὶ περὶ οἰκίας,

There is a story that some strangers from out of town once came to visit the philosopher Heraclitus, and when they found him warming himself by the bread oven, they stopped short at the door, whereupon Heraclitus said, "Take heart! Come on in! For there are gods here, too!"[1] Just so, we, too, ought to enter into research on every kind of animal with no fear or squeamishness since all of them contain Nature and possess Beauty. I add "Beauty" because it is purpose and not chance that is most at work in Nature, and the purpose for which animals have been formed or the end for which they have been created takes its place among what counts as beautiful.

If, however, someone has concluded that the study of animals is an undistinguished pursuit, on that same logic he ought to think the same about the study of himself. For it's impossible to look on the components from which a human being is constructed—blood, flesh, bones, veins, and so on—without a good deal of disgust. Relatedly, we should understand that someone who discusses any of these individual parts and their arrangements is not describing their material composition for its own sake but is concerned rather with the conformation of a whole. The same is true of a

ἀλλὰ μὴ πλίνθων καὶ πηλοῦ καὶ ξύλων· καὶ τὸν περὶ φύσεως περὶ τῆς συνθέσεως καὶ τῆς ὅλης οὐσίας, ἀλλὰ μὴ περὶ τούτων ἃ μὴ συμβαίνει χωριζόμενά ποτε τῆς οὐσίας αὐτῶν.

house—it's the whole structure that matters, not the bricks, mortar, and timber. Likewise, too, in Nature—the objective is to describe the synthetic whole, not the individual parts that do not occur separately apart from their combination as an entity.

2. People Are Animals Too (Aesopic Fables as Versified by Babrius)

One of the last things Socrates was working on be-fore the Athenians killed him was turning certain of Aesop's fables into verse (Plato, Phaedo *60d–61c). A man named Babrius, translated here, but about whom nothing is known except that he seems to have been a Roman from Syria writing in the second half of the first century CE, realized Socrates's ambition with considerable charm.*

Animal fables circulating under the name of Aesop became popular vehicles for communicating philosophical and political ideas beginning in the sixth century BCE. Aesop himself was reportedly an enslaved person from Thrace, owned by a man called Iadmon of Samos. The politics that his sto-ries reflect are decidedly Machiavellian. They ex-hort listeners to keep to their own station because, ultimately, "might makes right." One could be forgiven for thinking that such a view might have

HOW TO CARE ABOUT ANIMALS

Λύκος ποτ᾽ ἄρνα πεπλανημένον ποίμνης
ἰδὼν βίῃ μὲν οὐκ ἐπῆλθεν ἁρπάξων,
ἔγκλημα δ᾽ ἔχθρης εὐπρόσωπον ἐζήτει.
"σὺ δή με πέρυσι μικρὸς ὢν ἐβλασφήμεις."
5   "ἐγώ σε πέρυσιν; οὐκ ἐπ᾽ ἔτος ἐγεννήθην."
"οὔκουν σὺ τὴν ἄρουραν ἣν ἔχω κείρεις;"
"οὔπω τι χλωρὸν ἔφαγον οὐδ᾽ ἐβοσκήθην."
"οὐδ᾽ ἄρα πηγὴν ἐκπέπωκας ἣν πίνω;"
"θηλὴ μεθύσκει μέχρι νῦν με μητρῴη."
10 τότε δὴ τὸν ἄρνα συλλαβών τε καὶ τρώγων
"ἀλλ᾽ οὐκ ἄδειπνον" εἶπε "τὸν λύκον θήσεις,
κἂν εὐχερῶς μου πᾶσαν αἰτίην λύσῃς.

*been a smart survival strategy for someone like
Aesop. Even so, glimpses of subversion, or at least
of the possibility for social change, appear through
the cracks. Ultimately, though, it is human folly,
in all its rich variety, that is on full display in the
animal interactions here.*

The Wolf and the Lamb (No. 89)

A wolf once saw a lamb that had wandered off
from the flock, but he did not rush right at it to
snatch it away by force. Instead, he looked for a
plausible excuse to justify his enmity.

—"A year ago, small though you be, you
slandered me."

—"I slandered you last year? I haven't been
born a year!"

—"Well, aren't you chomping a field that is
my domain?"

—"No, I haven't yet begun to eat any grass or
to graze."

—"Haven't you drunk from the spring that is
mine, then?"

—"No, my mother's teat still provides me
with all that I drink."

Ὄνον τις ἔτρεφε καὶ κυνίδιον ὡραῖον,
τὸ κυνίδιον δ᾽ ἔχαιρε παῖζον εὐρύθμως,
τὸν δεσπότην τε ποικίλως περισκαῖρον·
κἀκεῖνος <αὖ> κατεῖχεν αὐτὸ τοῖς κόλποις.
5 ὁ δ᾽ ὄνος γ᾽ ἔκαμνεν ἑσπέρης ἀλετρεύων
πυρὸν φίλης Δήμητρος, ἡμέρης δ᾽ ὕλην
κατῆγ᾽ ἀφ᾽ ὕψους, ἐξ ἀγροῦ θ᾽ ὅσων χρείη·
καὶ μὴν ἐν αὐλῇ παρὰ φάτναισι δεσμώτης
ἔτρωγε κριθὰς χόρτον, ὥσπερ εἰώθει.
10 δηχθεὶς δὲ θυμῷ καὶ περισσὸν οἰμώξας,
σκύμνον θεωρῶν ἁβρότητι σὺν πάσῃ,
φάτνης ὀνείης δεσμὰ καὶ κάλους ῥήξας
ἐς μέσον αὐλῆς ἦλθ᾽ ἄμετρα λακτίζων.
σαίνων δ᾽ ὁποῖα καὶ θέλων περισκαίρειν,
15 τὴν μὲν τράπεζαν ἔθλασ᾽ ἐς μέσον βάλλων
ἅπαντα δ᾽ εὐθὺς ἡλόησε τὰ σκεύη·
δειπνοῦντα δ᾽ ἰθὺς ἦλθε δεσπότην κύσσων,
νώτοις ἐπεμβάς· ἐσχάτου δὲ κινδύνου
θεράποντες ἐν μέσοισιν ὡς <τὸν ἄνδρ᾽> εἶδον,

Whereupon the wolf snatched the lamb anyhow and, as he was munching him down, remarked: "You will not leave the wolf without his dinner, even if you find it easy to refute all my charges."

The Donkey and the Little Dog (No. 129)

A certain man kept a donkey and a cute little dog. The dog loved to play and did so with style. With great charm he would jump up and down all over his master. The master in turn cuddled the little dog on his lap. The donkey, however, spent his evenings toiling away grinding wheat, the gift of goodly Demeter. During the day he'd bring firewood down from the hills and whatever else was needed from the fields. Even in the courtyard he was chained like a prisoner to his stall to munch his barleycorn day after day. Eventually, seeing the puppy enjoying every luxury stung the donkey to the core. Bewailing his lot even more than usual, he broke the ropes and bonds that tied him to his ass's stall and sprang into the house, kicking up his hooves clumsily. He, too, wanted to fawn on the master and prance about like the little dog. He bolted inside, knocking over a table, and soon smashed all the furniture. The master

20 ἐσάωσαν <αὐτὸν ἐξ ὄνου γνάθων ὄντως>·
    κρανέης δὲ κορύναις ἄλλος ἄλλοθεν κρούων
    ἔθεινον, ὥστε καὐτὸς ὕστατ᾽ ἐκπνείων
    "ἔτλην" ἔλεξεν "οἷα χρή με, δυσδαίμων·
    τί γὰρ παρ᾽ οὐρήεσσιν οὐκ ἐπωλεύμην,
25 βαιῷ δ᾽ ὁ μέλεος κυνιδίῳ παρισούμην:"

    Γέννημα φρύνου συνεπάτησε βοῦς πίνων.
    ἐλθοῦσα δ᾽ αὐτόν—οὐ παρῆν γάρ—ἡ μήτηρ
    παρὰ τῶν ἀδελφῶν ποῦ ποτ᾽ ἦν ἐπεζήτει.
    "τέθνηκε, μῆτερ· ἄρτι γὰρ πρὸ τῆς ὥρης
5   ἦλθεν πάχιστον τετράπουν, ὑφ᾽ οὗ κεῖται
    χηλῇ μαλαχθείς." ἡ δὲ φρῦνος ἠρώτα,
    φυσῶσ᾽ ἑαυτήν, εἰ τοιοῦτον ἦν ὄγκῳ
    τὸ ζῷον. οἱ δὲ μητρί· "παῦε, μὴ πρήθου.
    θᾶσσον σεαυτήν," εἶπον, "ἐκ μέσου ῥήξεις
10 ἢ τὴν ἐκείνου ποιότητα μιμήσῃ."

himself was in the middle of eating his dinner. The donkey made right at him, intent on kissing him, then clambered up onto his back. The servants saw that their master was on the brink of disaster and saved him, as it were, from the jaws of an ass: One after another they pummeled and pounded the donkey with wooden clubs until he, breathing his last, said: "I've suffered what needs must, ill-fated as ever. Why did I not just carry on with the mules, instead of putting myself on par with a little dog, all in vain?"

All Puffed Up and Nowhere to Go (No. 28)

An ox took a sip of water and happened to step on a baby toad. When the mother toad returned (for she had been away), she asked the toad's siblings where on earth the baby toad was. "She's dead, Mother. Just moments ago, within the hour, a huge four-footed beast came along and crushed her under his hoof." The mother toad puffed herself out and asked if the animal was as big as *that* in girth. The sibling toads replied: "Mother, stop!" they said. "Don't overinflate yourself. Let yourself go. You will burst in the middle before you could ever match the capacity of that beast!"

Κόραξ δεδηχὼς στόματι τυρὸν εἱστήκει·
τυροῦ δ᾽ ἀλώπηξ ἰχανῶσα κερδῴη
μύθῳ τὸν ὄρνιν ἠπάτησε τοιούτῳ·
"κόραξ, καλαί σοι πτέρυγες, ὀξέη γλήνη,
5   θεητὸς αὐχήν· στέρνον αἰετοῦ φαίνεις,
ὄνυξι πάντων θηρίων κατισχύεις·
ὁ τοῖος ὄρνις κωφός ἐσσι κοὐ κρώζεις."
κόραξ δ᾽ ἐπαίνῳ καρδίην ἐχαυνώθη,
στόματος δὲ τυρὸν ἐκβαλὼν ἐκεκράγει.
10 τὸν ἡ σοφὴ λαβοῦσα κερτόμῳ γλώσσῃ
"οὐκ ἦσθ᾽ ἄφωνος" εἶπεν "ἀλλὰ φωνήεις·
ἔχεις, κόραξ, ἅπαντα, νοῦς δέ σοι λείπει."

Ὄρνιθος ἀγαθῆς ᾠὰ χρυσᾶ τικτούσης
ὁ δεσπότης ἐνόμισεν ἐντὸς εὑρήσειν
χρυσοῦ μέγιστον ὄγκον, ὅνπερ ὠδίνειν·
θύσας δὲ ταύτην εὗρε τὴν φύσιν πάσαις
5   <τὰ πάνθ᾽> ὁμοίην <οὖσαν. ἀθρόως δ᾽ ἕξειν>
μέγιστον ὄλβον ἐλπίσας τε καὶ σπεύσας
ἀπεστερήθη τοῦ τὰ μικρὰ κερδαίνειν.

The Fox and the Crow (No. 77)

A crow was standing on its perch, holding a chunk of cheese in his beak. A crafty fox, though, craved that cheese and tricked the bird with a speech that went something like this: "Crow, your wings are beautiful! Your eye is sharp! Your neck a sight to see! You have the chest of an eagle and those talons—why you could prevail over all other beasts with those! And yet, although a bird of such caliber, you are mute and don't caw?" The crow, puffed up in its heart by this praise, let out a loud "Caw!" and the cheese chunk fell from its mouth. The wily fox snatched it up and, wagging its tongue, said mockingly: "Ah, so you're not mute, after all, but can speak! You've got everything, Crow, but brains!"

The Hen That Laid Golden Eggs (No. 123)

A good hen had been laying golden eggs. So, her owner reckoned he would find a big pile of gold inside her, with which she was obviously pregnant. But after killing her he found her nature to be the same as that of all other hens. Hoping to get great wealth all at once and by being hasty about it, he wound up depriving himself of small gains.

21

Βότρυς μελαίνης ἀμπέλου παρωρείη
ἀπεκρέμαντο. τοὺς δὲ ποικίλη πλήρεις
ἰδοῦσα κερδὼ πολλάκις μὲν ὡρμήθη
πηδῶσα ποσσὶν πορφυρῆς θιγεῖν ὥρης·
5 ἦν γὰρ πέπειρος κεὶς τρυγητὸν ἀκμαίη.
κάμνουσα δ᾽ ἄλλως, οὐ γὰρ ἴσχυε ψαύειν,
παρῆλθεν οὕτω βουκολοῦσα τὴν λύπην·
"ὄμφαξ ὁ βότρυς, οὐ πέπειρος, ὡς ᾤμην."

Δυσμαὶ μὲν ἦσαν Πλειάδων, σπόρου δ᾽ ὥρη,
καί τις γεωργὸς πυρὸν εἰς νεὸν ῥίψας
ἐφύλασσεν ἑστώς· καὶ γὰρ ἄκριτον πλήθει
μέλαν κολοιῶν ἔθνος ἦλθε δυσφώνων
5 ψᾶρές τ᾽ ὄλεθρος σπερμάτων ἀρουραίων.
τῷ δ᾽ ἠκολούθει σφενδόνην ἔχων κοίλην
παιδίσκος. οἱ δὲ ψᾶρες ἐκ συνηθείης
ἤκουον εἰ τὴν σφενδόνην ποτ᾽ ἠτήκει,
καὶ πρὶν βαλεῖν ἔφευγον. εὗρε δὴ τέχνην
10 ὁ γεωργὸς ἄλλην τόν τε παῖδα φωνήσας
ἐδίδασκεν· "ὦ παῖ, χρὴ γὰρ ὀρνέων ἤμας
σοφὸν δολῶσαι φῦλον, ἡνίκ᾽ ἂν τοίνυν

The Fox and the Grapes (No. 19)

Some clusters of grapes were hanging down from a dark-colored vine on a hillside. A resourceful fox, seeing that they looked juicy, set herself to jumping up again and again on her hind feet to try to grasp the purple vintage, for the grapes were ripe and ready for harvest. Wearing herself out, with nothing gained, unable to reach them, she strutted away, nursing her disappointment with these words: "Those grapes were probably sour anyway, not ripe as I thought they were."

For the Birds (No. 33)

The Pleiades were setting, and it was the time for sowing. A farmer tossed his wheat seed into fresh ground and stood guard over it, for a flock of noisy black daws had swooped down in countless throng, starlings, too, to plunder the fields he had sown. A boy followed behind him holding an empty slingshot, but the starlings, accustomed to the farmer's voice, heard him whenever he called for the sling and fled before he could shoot at them. So, the farmer discovered a different technique and taught it to the boy, saying, "Boy, we must outsmart this clever tribe of birds. The next

ἔλθωσ᾽, ἐγὼ μέν," εἶπεν, "ἄρτον αἰτήσω,
σὺ δ᾽ οὐ τὸν ἄρτον, σφενδόνην δέ μοι δώσεις."
15   οἱ ψᾶρες ἦλθον κἀνέμοντο τὴν χώρην.
ὁ δ᾽ ἄρτον ᾔτει, καθάπερ εἶχε συνθήκην·
οἱ δ᾽ οὐκ ἔφευγον. τῷ δ᾽ ὁ παῖς λίθων πλήρη
τὴν σφενδόνην ἔδωκεν· ὁ δὲ γέρων ῥίψας
τοῦ μὲν τὸ βρέγμα, τοῦ δ᾽ ἔτυψε τὴν κνήμην,
20   ἑτέρου τὸν ὦμον, οἱ δ᾽ ἔφευγον ἐκ χώρης.
γέρανοι συνήντων καὶ τὸ συμβὰν ἠρώτων.
καί τις κολοιῶν εἶπε· "φεύγετ᾽ ἀνθρώπων
γένος πονηρόν, ἄλλα μὲν πρὸς ἀλλήλους
λαλεῖν μαθόντων, ἄλλα δ᾽ ἔργα ποιούντων."

Δαμάλης ἐν ἀγροῖς ἄφετος, ἀτριβὴς ζεύγλης,
κάμνοντι καὶ σύροντι τὴν ὕνιν ταύρῳ
"τάλας" ἐφώνει "μόχθον οἷον ὀτλεύεις."
ὁ βοῦς δ᾽ ἐσίγα χὐπέτεμνε τὴν χώρην.
5   ἐπεὶ δ᾽ ἔμελλον ἀγρόται θεοῖς θύειν,
ὁ βοῦς μὲν ὁ γέρων εἰς νομὰς ἀπεζεύχθη,
ὁ δὲ μόσχος ἀδμὴς κεῖνος εἵλκετο σχοίνῳ
δεθεὶς κέρατα, βωμὸν αἵματος πλήσων.
κἀκεῖνος αὐτῷ τοιάδ᾽ εἶπε φωνήσας·
10   "εἰς ταῦτα μέντοι μὴ πονῶν ἐτηρήθης.
ὁ νέος παρέρπεις τὸν γέροντα, καὶ θύῃ,
καὶ σοῦ τένοντα πέλεκυς, οὐ ζυγὸς τρίψει."

time they come I will ask for bread, but you give me not bread, but the sling." The starlings showed up and started pecking away at the field. The man called for bread, according to plan. The birds did not flee. The boy gave him the sling full of stones and the old man let fly, hitting one bird on the forehead, one in the shin, another in the shoulder, and off they fled from that place. Some cranes met up with them and asked what had happened. One of the daws said, "Flee from this foul tribe of humans! They have learned to say one thing to each other but do quite another."

The Old Bull and the Young Steer (No. 37)

A steer who had been turned out to pasture, who never had felt a yoke chafing on his neck, shouted to a bull who was toiling away, drawing a plough. "You miserable creature, what drudgery you endure!" The bull kept silent and went on cutting the ground. But when the country folk took to preparing a sacrifice for the gods, the old ox was unyoked and put out to pasture, whereas the young steer, who'd never experienced the yoke, was tied by the horns, and dragged along by a rope to stain the altar with his blood. The old bull shouted over to him and said, "It was for this, you

Λέων τις ἐβασίλευεν οὐχὶ θυμώδης
οὐδ᾽ ὠμὸς οὐδὲ πάντα τῇ βίῃ χαίρων,
πρηῢς δὲ καὶ δίκαιος ὥς τις ἀνθρώπων.
ἐπὶ τῆς ἐκείνου φασὶ δὴ δυναστείης
5   τῶν ἀγρίων ἀγυρμὸς ἐγεγόνει ζῴων,
δίκας τε δοῦναι καὶ λαβεῖν παρ᾽ ἀλλήλων.
τὰ ζῷα πάντα δ᾽ ὡς ὑπέσχον εὐθύνας,
λύκος μὲν ἀρνί, πάρδαλις δ᾽ ἐπ᾽ αἰγάγρῳ,
ἐλάφῳ δὲ τίγρις, πάντα δ᾽ εἶχεν εἰρήνην,
10   ὁ πτὼξ λαγωὸς εἶπεν "ἀλλ᾽ ἐγὼ ταύτην
τὴν ἡμέρην ἀεί ποτ᾽ ηὐχόμην, ἥτις
καὶ τοῖς βιαίοις φοβερὰ τἀσθενῆ θήσει."

see, you were coddled, not having to work. You are young, yet you shamble along ahead of me, an old bull, on death's road. You will be sacrificed. An axe, not the yoke, will bear down on *your* neck."

Peaceable Kingdom (No. 102)

A lion came to be king, but he was not aggressive or bloodthirsty, nor fond of using violence to settle everything, but was gentle and just, as a human might be. They say that during his reign the wild animals met in assembly to give and to receive legal verdicts from one another. All the animals were held to account for their deeds—the wolf by the lamb, the leopard by the mountain goat, the tiger by the deer, and they all settled their affairs in peace. The cowering hare said, "Well, I'll be! This is the day I have long prayed for without ceasing, one that will make the weak animals feared by the strong."

3. My Octopus Teacher
(Theognis, Lines 213–18)

Theognis was an aristocrat from Megara, a Greek city in the Peloponnese. He flourished in the sixth century BCE. About fifteen hundred lines of lyric verse composed in elegiacs have come down to us attributed to him. Theognis's poetry is topical and moralizing, and it reflects the sociopolitical tensions of his time. The lines excerpted and translated here, which recommend adopting the cagey behavior of the octopus in human social relations, probably depend on observational knowledge derived from ancient Greek sponge divers.

HOW TO CARE ABOUT ANIMALS

θυμέ, φίλους κατὰ πάντας ἐπίστρεφε ποικίλον
    ἦθος,
        ὀργὴν συμμίσγων ἥντιν' ἕκαστος ἔχει.
πουλύπου ὀργὴν ἴσχε πολυπλόκου, ὃς ποτὶ
    πέτρῃ,
        τῇ προσομιλήσῃ, τοῖος ἰδεῖν ἐφάνη.
νῦν μὲν τῇδ' ἐφέπου, τότε δ' ἀλλοῖος χρόα
    γίνου.
        κρέσσων τοι σοφίη γίνεται ἀτροπίης.

MY OCTOPUS TEACHER

Display a varied cast of mind, my heart,
among all your friends. Mingle with the
   mood
that each one's got. Adopt the attitude
of an octopod, who by complex art
takes on the look of the rock it clings to.
Apply one shade now, now a different hue.
Don't be static. It's better to be smart.[1]

4. The Quality of Mercy
(Aulus Gellius, *Attic Nights* 5.14)

George Bernard Shaw was sufficiently moved by the story of Androcles and the Lion to write a play about it. Shaw casts the slave Androcles as a condemned Christian and the Lion as, well, a lion. His preface to the play, which is longer than the play itself, consists of a polemical reassessment of the teachings of Jesus as preserved in the four Gospels. When Jesus declares "Go and learn what this means: 'I desire mercy and not sacrifice'" (Matthew 9:13, quoting Hosea 6:6), the Son of Man's intent, according to Shaw, is "to clear himself of the inveterate superstition that suffering is gratifying to God." Shaw was so attached to the Androcles story that he specified in his will that a lion's share of his estate should be spent on transliterating Androcles and the Lion *into the Shavian alphabet, which he had devised to replace the Roman one. Penguin published the curious result in 1962.*

33

Apion, qui Plistonices appellatus est, litteris homo multis praeditus rerumque Graecarum plurima atque varia scientia fuit. Eius libri non incelebres feruntur, quibus omnium ferme quae mirifica in Aegypto visuntur audiunturque historia comprehenditur. Sed in his quae vel audisse vel legisse sese dicit, fortassean vitio studioque ostentationis sit loquacior—est enim sane quam in praedicandis doctrinis sui venditator—hoc autem, quod in libro Aegyptiacorum quinto scripsit, neque audisse neque legisse, sed ipsum sese in urbe Roma vidisse oculis suis confirmat.

"In Circo Maximo," inquit, "venationis amplissimae, pugna populo dabatur. Eius rei, Romae cum forte essem, spectator," inquit, "fui. Multae

THE QUALITY OF MERCY

Aulus Gellius's version of the story, translated here, via a raconteur named Apion, has no Christians in it, but plenty of mercy. Gellius (ca. 125–ca. 180 CE) was a Roman grammarian and antiquarian, whose commonplace book Attic Nights *was the studious result of winter evenings the author spent as an expat living in the countryside around Athens—the perfect mise-en-scène for this heartwarming tale.*

Apion, surnamed Plistonices, was learned and possessed a good deal of miscellaneous knowledge of things Greek. His books, which constitute an account of nearly all the marvels to be seen or ascertained from hearsay in Egypt, are quite well known. In the accounts of what he says he has seen or read he is perhaps too wordy—a fault attributable to his eagerness to show off. Apion is, to be sure, quite the salesman when it comes to peddling his learning. But this marvel below, from the fifth book of his *Wonders of Egypt*, he insists he didn't just hear or read about secondhand but saw himself with his own eyes in the city of Rome.

"In the Circus Maximus," he says,[1] "a gladiatorial show involving an impressive horde of wild animals was being put on for the People.

ibi saevientes ferae, magnitudines bestiarum excellentes omniumque invisitata aut forma erat aut ferocia. Sed praeter alia omnia leonum," inquit, "immanitas admirationi fuit praeterque omnis ceteros unus. Is unus leo corporis impetu et vastitudine terrificoque fremitu et sonoro, toris comisque cervicum fluctuantibus, animos oculosque omnium in sese converterat.

Introductus erat inter compluris ceteros ad pugnam bestiarum datos[1] servus viri consularis; ei servo Androclus nomen fuit. Hunc ille leo ubi vidit procul, repente," inquit, "quasi admirans stetit ac deinde sensim atque placide, tamquam noscitabundus, ad hominem accedit. Tum caudam more atque ritu adulantium canum clementer et blande movet hominisque se corpori adiungit cruraque eius et manus, prope iam exanimati metu, lingua leniter demulcet. Homo Androclus inter illa tam atrocis ferae blandimenta amissum animum recuperat, paulatim oculos ad contuendum leonem refert. Tum quasi mutua recognitione facta laetos," inquit, "et gratulabundos videres hominem et leonem."

THE QUALITY OF MERCY

I happened to be in Rome at the time and so was a spectator at this event. There were many ferocious beasts there, larger than most wild animals, and notable for their unusual forms or fierceness. But exceeding all others were the lions. Their enormous size was a wonder to behold, and one lion was exceptional beyond the rest. This lion attracted attention and turned all eyes toward himself on account of his physical size and speed, his terrifying, resounding roar, his rippling muscles, and the mane cascading down his neck.

"Among many other men condemned to fight with the animals a slave belonging to a man of consular rank was brought into the arena. His name was Androcles. The lion caught sight of him from a distance, but then, suddenly, stopped in his tracks, seemingly astounded. He slowly and calmly approached Androcles, who was himself almost already dead from fear, as if he recognized him. He gave his tail a cheery, friendly wag, as dogs that are eager to please are wont to do, embraced Androcles, and began gently to lick his hands and feet with his tongue. Such fawning by such a fearsome beast inspired Androcles, the human party, to regain the courage he had lost. Little by little, he turned his gaze to look the lion

Ea re prorsus tam admirabili maximos populi clamores excitatos dicit, accersitumque a C. Caesare Androclum quaesitamque causam cur illi atrocissimus leo uni parsisset. Ibi Androclus rem mirificam narrat atque admirandam.

"Cum provinciam," inquit, "Africam proconsulari imperio meus dominus obtineret, ego ibi iniquis eius et cotidianis verberibus ad fugam sum coactus et, ut mihi a domino, terrae illius praeside, tutiores latebrae forent, in camporum et arenarum solitudines concessi ac, si defuisset cibus, consilium fuit mortem aliquo pacto quaerere. Tum sole medio," inquit, "rabido et flagranti specum quandam nanctus remotam latebrosamque, in eam me penetro et recondo. Neque multo post ad eandem specum venit hic leo, debili uno et cruento pede, gemitus edens et murmura, dolorem cruciatumque vulneris commiserantia."

in the face, and, when he did, you would have thought you were watching a joyful exchange of greetings between friends that had recognized one another—a lion and a man!"

Apion then says the crowd erupted with loud cheers at such an astonishing sight, whereupon Gaius Caesar had Androcles summoned to ask him why a most dreadful lion had spared him and him alone. At which point in the story Androcles relates a wondrous, extraordinary tale.

"My master was serving as governor of the province of Africa," he began, "and it was there, because of the daily and undeserved beatings I received, that I was forced to become a fugitive. I took to the empty desert expanses so that my hideouts might be safer from my master since he presided over that territory. And if a source of food were to fail me there, I had made up my mind to seek death by some method of my own contriving. At one point, when the sun was scorching, hot, and fierce at midday, I stumbled upon a remote and sheltered cave, entered it, and hid myself there. Not long after, this lion came in, too, one of his paws injured and bloody, moaning and groaning forth pleas for compassion for the excruciating pain of his wound."

Atque illic primo quidem conspectu advenien-
tis leonis territum sibi et pavefactum animum
dixit. "Sed postquam introgressus," inquit, "leo,
uti re ipsa apparuit, in habitaculum illud suum,
videt me procul delitescentem, mitis et mansues
accessit et sublatum pedem ostendere mihi et
porgere quasi opis petendae gratia visus est. Ibi,"
inquit, "ego stirpem ingentem, vestigio pedis eius
haerentem, revelli conceptamque saniem volnere
intimo expressi accuratiusque sine magna iam for-
midine siccavi penitus atque detersi cruorem. Illa
tunc mea opera et medella levatus, pede in manibus meis posito, recubuit et quievit atque ex eo die
triennium totum ego et leo in eadem specu eo-
demque et victu viximus. Nam, quas venabatur
feras, membra opimiora ad specum mihi subgere-
bat, quae ego, ignis copiam non habens, meridi-
ano sole torrens edebam.

Sed ubi me," inquit, "vitae illius ferinae iam
pertaesum est, leone in venatum profecto, reliqui
specum et viam ferme tridui permensus a militi-
bus visus adprehensusque sum et ad dominum ex
Africa Romam deductus. Is me statim rei capi-
talis damnandum dandumque ad bestias curavit.

Androcles said his mind went numb with fear and dread as soon as he caught sight of the lion approaching. "But," he continued, "once the lion had entered what was, the facts seemed to suggest, his own lair, and saw me cowering at a distance, he drew near, softly and gently, then, raising his paw, seemed to extend it out for me to look at as if for the purpose of seeking help. Lo and behold, there was a huge splinter lodged in the sole of his foot. I removed it, squeezed out the pus that had formed inside the wound, and then, my great fear now abating, dried it very carefully and thoroughly, wiping away the blood. Put at ease by my work of healing, the lion placed his paw in my hands, lay down, and fell asleep. For three whole years from that day the lion and I lived in that same cave, on the same food, for he would bring back to the cave the choicest parts of the prey he hunted for me to eat, which I dried in the noonday sun, since I had no supplies to make a fire.

"Eventually I became tired of that feral way of life, so while the lion was out hunting, I left the cave, only to be seen and apprehended by soldiers, three days' journey later, on the open road. I was taken from Africa to Rome, back to my master, who immediately saw to it that I was condemned

Intellego autem," inquit, "hunc quoque leonem, me tunc separato captum, gratiam mihi nunc beneficii et medicinae referre."

Haec Apion dixisse Androclum tradit, eaque omnia scripta circumlataque tabula populo declarata, atque ideo cunctis petentibus dimissum Androclum et poena solutum leonemque ei suffragiis populi donatum. "Postea," inquit, "videbamus Androclum et leonem, loro tenui revinctum, urbe tota circum tabernas ire, donari aere Androclum, floribus spargi leonem, omnes ubique obvios dicere: 'Hic est leo hospes hominis, hic est homo medicus leonis.'"

to death by being tossed to the wild beasts. I take it that this lion here, too, was captured after I left, and that he is now returning me the favor for my kindness and ministrations."

This was the story that Apion reports Androcles told, and that when the whole of it had been written out and circulated among the People on a tablet, everyone petitioned the emperor to have Androcles released and acquitted, and, by popular vote, to be given the lion as a gift. "Afterward," he adds, "we used to see Androcles with his lion tied to a flimsy leash promenading through the city, making the rounds to the shops; Androcles was gifted money, the lion sprinkled with flowers, and everyone who crossed their path would say 'This is the lion, a human's friend; this is the human, a lion's doctor.'"

5. Escape Artists
(Selections from Aelian, *The Peculiar Behaviors of Animals*)

Claudius Aelianus, or just "Aelian" (ca. 175–
ca. 235 CE), was a Roman litterateur who wrote in
Greek. His sprawling work on animals in seven-
teen books, sometimes called The Characteristics
of Animals, *or* De Natura Animalium, *is a trea-*
sure trove of miscellaneous information and sus-
pect fact that provided much of the material we
find in the medieval bestiaries. The selections
translated here highlight Aelian's interest in ani-
mals that get away, either from predators or from
other dangers in their natural environments.
There is just a touch of Aesop in his characteriza-
tions of these crafty escape artists.

Οἱ κοχλίαι ἴσασιν εἶναί σφισι πολεμίους τοὺς πέρδικας καὶ τοὺς ἐρῳδιούς, καὶ αὐτοὺς ἀποδιδρά-
σκουσιν, οὐδ᾽ ἂν ἴδοις ἔνθα οὗτοι νέμονται κοχλίας
διέρποντας. οἱ δὲ καλούμενοι τῶν κοχλιῶν ἀρείο-
νες, οὗτοι μὲν καὶ ἀπατῶσι καὶ περιέρχονταί τινι
φυσικῇ σοφίᾳ τοὺς προειρημένους. τῶν γὰρ συμ-
φυῶν ὀστράκων προελθόντες αὐτοὶ μὲν νέμονται
κατὰ πολλὴν τὴν ἄδειαν, οἱ δὲ ὄρνιθες οὓς εἶπον
ἐπὶ τὰ κενὰ τῶν ὀστράκων ὡς ἐπ᾽ αὐτοὺς ἐκεί-
νους καταπέτονται, οὐδὲν δὲ εὑρόντες ἀπέρριψαν
ὡς ἀχρεῖά σφισι καὶ ἀνεχώρησαν· οἱ δὲ ἐπανελθό-
ντες εἶτα ἕκαστος ἐς τὴν ἰδίαν οἰκίαν παρῆλθε,
κεκορεσμένος μὲν ἐκ τῆς νομῆς, σωθεὶς δὲ ἐξ ἧς
ἠπάτησε πλάνης.

Θυμόσοφα δὲ καὶ παρ᾽ ἡμῖν ζῷά ἐστιν, οὐ μὴν ὅσα
ἐν Ἰνδοῖς ἀλλὰ ὀλίγα. ἐκεῖ δὲ ὅ τε ἐλέφας τοιοῦτός
ἐστι καὶ ὁ σιττακὸς καὶ αἱ σφίγγες καὶ οἱ καλούμενοι σάτυροι· σοφὸν δὲ ἄρα ἦν καὶ ὁ μύρμηξ ὁ Ἰνδός.
οἱ μὲν οὖν ἡμεδαποὶ τὰς ἑαυτῶν χειὰς καὶ ὑποδρο-
μὰς ὑπὸ τὴν γῆν ὀρύττουσι, καὶ φωλεούς τινας
κρυπτοὺς ἀποφαίνουσι γεωρυχοῦντες, καὶ μεταλ-
λείαις ὡς εἰπεῖν τισιν ἀπορρήτοις καὶ λανθανούσαις

Snails (10.5)

Snails know that partridges and herons are their enemies, so they flee from them. You won't see snails creeping about where these birds feed. Those snails that are called "The Better Ones," however, the Areiones, deceive and circumvent said birds by an innate cleverness. These snails, you see, crawl out of the shells in which they live and grow to graze for food carefree, while the birds that I mentioned swoop down on the empty shells as if there were snails in them. Finding nothing, the birds toss the shells aside as useless and fly away. Whereupon, the Areiones return, each to his own house, sated from their grazing and saved by their deceitful walkabout.

Ants (16.15)

We have our share of intelligent animals, but few compared to the number they have in India. There you'll find of such a sort the elephant, the parrot, sphinxes, and so-called satyrs.[1] And then of course there's the Indian ant,[2] who's also a clever creature. The ants of our country, to be sure, dig holes and tunnels for themselves underground to reveal hidden lairs where they wear themselves

καταξαίνονται·ἀλλὰ οἵ γε Ἰνδοὶ μύρμηκες οἰκί-
σκους τινὰς συμφορητοὺς ἐργάζονται, καὶ τούτους
γε οὐκ ἐν χωρίοις ὑπτίοις καὶ λείοις καὶ ἐπικλυζο-
μένοις ῥᾷστα, ἀλλὰ μετεώροις καὶ ὑψηλοῖς. ἐν
αὐτοῖς δὲ περιόδους τινὰς καὶ ὡς εἰπεῖν σύριγγας
Αἰγυπτίας ἢ λαβυρίνθους Κρητικοὺς σοφίᾳ τινὶ
ἀπορρήτῳ διατρήσαντες οἰκεῖα ἑαυτοῖς ἀπέφηναν,
οὐκ εὐθυτενῆ καὶ ῥᾴδια παρελθεῖν ἀλλ᾽ ἑλιγμοῖς
καὶ διατρήσεσι λοξά· καὶ ἀπολείπουσί γε ἐπιπολῆς
μίαν ὀπήν, δι᾽ ἧς εἰσίασί τε αὐτοὶ καὶ τὰ σπέρματα
ὅσα ἐκλέγουσι, εἶτα ἐς τοὺς ἑαυτῶν θησαυροὺς
ἐσκομίζουσι. παλαμῶνται δὲ ἄρα τὰς ἐν ὕψει φω-
λεύσεις ὑπὲρ τοῦ τὰς ἐκ τῶν ποταμῶν ἀναχύσεις
τε καὶ ἐπικλύσεις διαδιδράσκειν. καὶ αὐτοῖς ὑπὲρ
τῆσδε τῆς σοφίας περιγίνεται ὥσπερ ἐν σκοπιαῖς
τισιν ἢ νήσοις κατοικεῖν, ὅταν τῶν λοφιδίων
ἐκείνων τὰ κύκλῳ περιλιμνάσῃ.

τὰ δ᾽ οὖν χώματα ἐκεῖνα, καίτοι συμπεφορη-
μένα, τοσοῦτον ἀποδεῖ τοῦ λύεσθαί τε καὶ
διαξαίνεσθαι ὑπὸ τῆς περικλύσεως, ὡς καὶ κρα-
τύνεσθαι αὐτά, πρῶτον μὲν ὑπὸ τῆς ἑῴας δρό-
σου· ὑπαμφιέννυται γὰρ ὡς εἰπεῖν ἐκ ταύτης
πάγου τινὰ χιτῶνα ὑπόλεπτον, πλὴν καρτερόν·

out as if engaged in secret, clandestine mining for ore. The ants of India, however, build little mansions out of gathered material above ground, not in flat, low-lying areas that would flood easily, but high aloft. Inside, by some secret skill, they bore passageways—one might say catacombs, like those in Egypt, or labyrinths, like the one on Crete—to make abodes for themselves—not with a direct approach, easy to pass through, but crooked, with twists and tunnels. At the top, however, they leave a single opening through which they enter carrying whatever seeds they've collected, which they then bring down to their storerooms. They construct their cave dwellings on high, one infers, to escape from the floods and deluges of rivers. Owing to this clever practice it's as if they inhabit watchtowers or islands whenever the area around their little hilltops is inundated.

What is more, their mounds, although constructed from aggregated material, far from being destroyed or washed away by flooding, are in fact strengthened, first by the morning dew, the hardened scum of which coats the mounds, as it were, with a fine, but strong cloak, and then also

εἶτα μέντοι δεσμεύεται κάτω βρυώδει τῆς ποταμίας
ἰλύος φλοιῷ.

Θεῖ δὲ ὁ λαγὼς ὑπό τε κυνῶν καὶ ἱππέων διωκόμε-
νος, εἰ μὲν ἐκ πεδιάδος γῆς εἴη, ὠκύτερον τῶν
ὀρείων λαγών, ἅτε μικρὸς τὸ σῶμα καὶ λεπτός·
ἔνθεν τοι καὶ κοῦφον αὐτὸν εἶναι οὐκ ἀπεικός.
σκιρτᾷ γοῦν τὰ πρῶτα ἀπὸ τῆς γῆς καὶ πηδᾷ, δια-
δύεται δὲ καὶ διὰ θάμνων ὀλισθηρῶς καὶ εὐκόλως
καὶ διὰ παντὸς ἑλώδους τόπου· καὶ εἴ που πόαι βα-
θεῖαι, καὶ διὰ τούτων διεκπίπτει ῥᾳδίως. καὶ ὅπερ
τοῖς λέουσί φασι τὴν ἀλκαίαν δύνασθαι πρὸς τὸ
ἐγείρειν αὐτοὺς καὶ ἐποτρύνειν, τοῦτό τοι καὶ
ἐκείνῳ τὰ ὦτά ἐστι, ῥύμης συνθήματα καὶ ἐγερ-
τήρια δρόμου. ἀνακλίνει γοῦν κατὰ τῶν νώτων
αὐτά, κέχρηται δὲ αὐτοῖς πρὸς τὸ μὴ ἐλινύειν μηδὲ
ὀκνεῖν οἷον μύωψι. δρόμον δὲ ἕνα καὶ εὐθὺν οὐ θεῖ,
δεῦρο δὲ καὶ ἐκεῖσε παρακλίνει, καὶ ἐξελίττει τῇ καὶ
τῇ, ἐκπλήττων τοὺς κύνας καὶ ἀπατῶν. ὅποι ποτὲ
δ᾽ ἂν ὁρμήσῃ καὶ ἀπονεῦσαι θελήσῃ, κατ᾽ ἐκείνην
τὴν ἐκτροπὴν κλίνει τῶν ὤτων τὸ ἕτερον, οἷον
ἰθύνων ἑαυτῷ διὰ τούτου τὸν δρόμον.

οὐ μὴν ἀναλίσκει τὴν ἑαυτοῦ δύναμιν ἀταμι-
εύτως, τηρεῖ δὲ τοῦ διώκοντος τὴν ὁρμήν, καὶ ἐὰν

they are bound fast at the base by a weedy bark
that is deposited by mud from the river.

Hares (13.14)

When chased by hounds and horsemen, the hare
runs, if it is the plains variety, faster than mountain hares, for its body is small and light. And so
of course it's no surprise that it's nimble. It leaps
and bounds from the ground at first, then scoots
through brambles and over marshy terrain with
slipperiness and ease. In places where the grass is
thick it gets away scot-free. And what people say
about the lion—that its tail can rouse and spur it
on—this is the function of the hare's ears, which
serve as signals of its quick motion and as an in-
ducement for its flight. At any rate, it bends them
back and uses them like goads to keep it from
slowing down or hesitating. However, its course
is neither single nor straight, but it darts this way
then that, zigzagging left and right, exasperating
the hounds with its feints. And in whatever direc-
tion it lurches and wishes to veer, it drops one of
its ears toward that path, as if it were steering its
course thereby.

However, it does not waste its strength. Rather,
it monitors the speed of its pursuer. If he is slow,

μὲν ᾖ νωθής, οὐ πᾶν ἀνῆκε τὸ ἑαυτοῦ τάχος, ἀλλά
τι καὶ ἀνέστειλεν, ὡς προεκθεῖν μὲν <τοῦ> κυνός,
οὐ μὴν ἀπαγορεῦσαι ὑπὸ τοῦ συντόνου τοῦ δρόμου
αὐτός. οἶδε γὰρ ἀμείνων ὤν, καὶ ὁρᾷ ἐς τὸ μὴ ὑπερ-
πονεῖσθαί οἱ τὸν καιρὸν ὄντα. ἐὰν δὲ καὶ ὁ κύων
ᾖ ὤκιστος, τηνικαῦτα ὁ λαγὼς φέρεται θέων ᾖ
ποδῶν ἔχει. ἤδη γοῦν καὶ πολὺ τῆς ὁδοῦ προλαβών,
καὶ ἀπολιπὼν ἐκ πολλοῦ θηρατὰς καὶ κύνας καὶ ἵπ-
πους, ἐπί τινα λόφον ὑψηλὸν ἀναθορὼν καὶ ἑαυτὸν ἀναστήσας ἐπὶ τῶν κατόπιν ποδῶν, οἷον ἀπὸ
σκοπιᾶς ὁρᾷ τὴν τῶν διωκόντων ἅμιλλαν, καί μοι
δοκεῖ ὡς ἀσθενεστέρων καταγελᾶν αὐτῶν. εἶτα ἐκ
τούτου θαρρήσας[1] ὡς πλέον ἔχων, οἷον εἰρήνης καὶ
γαλήνης λαβόμενος ἀσμένως ἡσυχάζει καὶ κεῖται
καθεύδων.

Οἱ στρουθοὶ οἱ σμικροὶ συνειδότες ἑαυτοῖς ἀσθέ-
νειαν διὰ σμικρότητα τοῦ σώματος, ἐπὶ τοῖς
ἀκρεμόσι τῶν κλάδων τοῖς φέρειν αὐτοὺς δυναμένοις τὰς νεοττιὰς συμπλάσαντες εἶτα μέντοι τὴν
ἐκ τῶν θηρατῶν ἐπιβουλὴν ὡς τὰ πολλὰ διαφεύ-
γουσιν ἐπιβῆναι τῷ κλαδὶ μὴ δυναμένων· οὐ γὰρ
αὐτοὺς φέρει διὰ λεπτότητα.

it does not unleash itself at full speed but holds back a bit—enough to outrun the hound, but not exhausting itself by an intense chase. For it knows it can do better and understands that this is not the time for overexerting itself. If, however, the hound is quite quick, then the hare runs as fast as its legs can carry it. Later on, when it's a good way ahead, having left hunters and hounds far behind, it darts up some high hill, where, perched on its hind legs, it surveys, as if from a lookout, the fracas of its pursuers and, it seems to me, laughs at them for being the weaker party in the chase. Then, emboldened by having gotten the better of them, and like someone who's found some peace and quiet, the hare is glad for his rest and lies down for a nap there.

Sparrows (4.38)

Sparrows are aware that they are weak because their bodies are small. So, they construct their nests on those twigs amid the branches that can support only them and so for the most part escape thereby the schemes of predators, who cannot climb on the branch, for it is too flimsy to support them.

HOW TO CARE ABOUT ANIMALS

Λύκοι ποταμὸν διανέοντες, ὑπὲρ τοῦ μὴ πρὸς βίαν ἐκ τῆς τοῦ ῥεύματος ἐμβολῆς ἀνατρέπεσθαι ἕρμα ἴδιον αὑτοῖς ἡ φύσις συμπλάσασα ἐδιδάξατο σωτηρίαν ἐξ ἀπόρων καὶ μάλα εὔπορον. τὰς οὐρὰς τὰς ἀλλήλων ἐνδακόντες, εἶτα ἀντιπίπτουσι τῷ ῥεύματι, καὶ ἀλύπως διενήξαντο καὶ ἀσφαλῶς.

Ὁ δὲ ναυτίλος πολύπους ἐστὶ καὶ αὐτός, καὶ κόγχην μίαν ἔχει. ἀναπλεῖ μὲν οὖν τὴν κόγχην στρέψας περὶ τὰ κάτω, ἵνα μὴ τῆς ἅλμης ἀρύσηται καὶ ὠθήσῃ αὖθις αὐτόν· γενόμενος δὲ ἐπὶ τοῖς κύμασιν, ὅταν μὲν ᾖ γαλήνη καὶ εἰρήνη πνευμάτων, στρέφει τὴν κόγχην ὑπτίαν (ἡ δὲ ἐπιπλεῖ δίκην πορθμίδος) καὶ παρεὶς δύο πλεκτάνας ἐντεῦθέν τε καὶ ἐκεῖθεν καὶ ὑποκινῶν ἡσυχῇ ἐρέττει τε καὶ προωθεῖ τὴν συμφυῆ ναῦν. εἰ δὲ εἴη πνεῦμα, τοὺς ἐρετμοὺς μὲν τοὺς τέως προτείνας μακροτέρους οἴακας ἐργάζεται, ἄλλας δὲ ἀνατείνας πλεκτάνας, ὧν μέσος χιτών ἐστι λεπτότατος, τοῦτον διαστήσας ἱστίον αὐτὸν ἀποφαίνει. πλεῖ μὲν δὴ τὸν τρόπον τοῦτον ἀδεὴς ὤν· ἐὰν μέντοι φοβηθῇ τι τῶν

Wolves (3.6)

Nature has devised for wolves a unique trick to prevent them from being violently swept away by the force of the current when they swim across a river, thus teaching them how to obtain safe and easy passage through an impasse: they sink their teeth into one another's tails, lean into the current, and thus swim to the other side unhampered and unharmed.

The Argonaut (9.34)

The Argonaut,[3] too, is an octopus, but it has a single shell. It rises up to the surface, turning its shell upside down so that it doesn't draw in sea water and get pushed back down again. Once on top of the waves, when the winds are calm and the weather is clear, its shell turned to face upward, it floats like a boat. Then, extending two tentacles, one on each side, and plying them gently, it rows and propels its ship, one formed from its own nature. If there's a breeze, it extends what, up till then, were oars and uses them as rudders. Then it hoists aloft other tentacles, between which is stretched a thin membrane, and, spreading this out, creates a sail and glides along in such fashion

ἁδροτέρων, βυθίσας τὴν κόγχην ἐπλήρωσε, καὶ κα-
τώλισθεν ἐκ τοῦ βάρους, καὶ ἑαυτὸν ἀφανίσας τὸν
ἐχθρὸν ἀπέδρα. εἶτα ἐν εἰρήνῃ γενόμενος ἀνέθορέ
τε καὶ πλεῖ πάλιν. καὶ ἐκ τούτων ἔχει τὸ ὄνομα.

Ὁ κάστωρ ἀμφίβιόν ἐστι ζῷον, καὶ μεθ' ἡμέραν
μὲν ἐν τοῖς ποταμοῖς καταδὺς διαιτᾶται, νύκτωρ δὲ
ἐπὶ τῆς γῆς ἀλᾶται, οἷς ἂν περιτύχῃ τούτοις τρεφό-
μενος. οὐκοῦν ἐπίσταται τὴν αἰτίαν δι' ἣν ἐπ' αὐτὸν
οἱ θηραταὶ σὺν προθυμίᾳ τε καὶ ὁρμῇ τῇ πάσῃ χω-
ροῦσι, καὶ ἐπικύψας καὶ δακὼν ἀπέκοψε τοὺς ἑαυτοῦ ὄρχεις, καὶ προσέρριψεν αὐτοῖς, ὡς ἀνὴρ
φρόνιμος λῃσταῖς μὲν περιπεσών, καταθεὶς δὲ ὅσα
ἐπήγετο ὑπὲρ τῆς ἑαυτοῦ σωτηρίας, λύτρα δήπου
ταῦτα ἀλλαττόμενος.

ἐὰν δὲ ᾖ πρότερον ἐκτεμὼν καὶ σωθεὶς εἶτα
πάλιν διώκηται, ὁ δὲ ἀναστήσας ἑαυτὸν καὶ ἐπιδεί-
ξας ὅτι τῆς αὐτῶν σπουδῆς οὐκ ἔχει τὴν ὑπόθεσιν,
τοῦ περαιτέρω καμάτου παρέλυσε τοὺς θηρατάς·
ἧττον γάρ τοι τῶν κρεῶν ἐκείνοις φροντίς ἐστι.
πολλάκις δὲ καὶ ἔνορχοι ὄντες, ὡς ὅτι πορρωτάτω

without fear. If, however, it becomes afraid of some larger creature, it fills its shell with water and so submerges because of the weight and evades its enemy by vanishing. Then, when the coast is clear, it shoots back up and sets sail once again. It's from these behaviors that it gets its name.

Beavers (6.34)

The beaver is an amphibious animal. During the day it passes its time in rivers, sunk below the surface. But at night it traipses about on land, nourishing itself with whatever it chances upon. Surely it knows the reason that hunters pursue it with all eagerness and such onslaught, for it bends forward, chews off its testicles, and tosses them in their path, just as a sensible man, when he falls among thieves, places before them all that he is carrying, exchanging it for his own deliverance, no doubt, as if it were a ransom.

If, however, a beaver is again pursued after saving himself by castration, he stands himself up to show that he is not in possession of what occasions their pursuit and thus relieves the hunters of further effort, for they are less fond of meat from a gelding.[4] Often, though, even fully

ἀποσπάσαντες τῷ δρόμῳ, εἶτα ὑποστείλαντες τὸ σπουδαζόμενον μέρος, πάνυ σοφῶς καὶ πανούργως ἐξηπάτησαν, ὡς οὐκ ἔχοντες ἃ κρύψαντες εἶχον.

testicled beavers, once they've scurried off as far as they can during a chase, retract their precious bits and thus deceive their pursuers with knavish finesse, pretending not to possess what they've really been keeping hidden.

6. Animal Spirits
(Seneca, *Letters* No. 60)

This short letter from Seneca to his friend Lucilius about misplaced prayers pulls out all the rhetorical stops to show how, in our overreach and greediness, we humans are ecologically inferior to our animal cousins. Nonhuman animals instinctively know and are satisfied with their place in Nature. We, by contrast, Seneca suggests (with a scathing etymological pun on the word animal*), are inanimates, like the living dead. In making this argument Seneca draws on the Stoic doctrine of* oikeiōsis, *an idea that anticipates the biologist Jakob von Uexküll's notion of* Umwelt, *a term he coined to describe an organism's awareness of its place in its environment, and which is now a key concept in modern biosemiotics. While the Delphic dictum "Know thyself" is tried and true as a philosophical tenet, so, too, is "Know thy place," as Seneca reminds us here.*

SENECA LUCILIO SUO SALUTEM:
Queror, litigo, irascor. Etiamnunc optas quod tibi optavit nutrix tua aut paedagogus aut mater? Nondum intellegis quantum mali optaverint? O quam inimica nobis sunt vota nostrorum! Eo quidem inimiciora quo cessere felicius. Iam non admiror si omnia nos a prima pueritia mala sequuntur; inter execrationes parentum crevimus. Exaudiant di nostram quoque pro nobis vocem gratuitam.

Quousque poscemus aliquid deos ita quasi nondum ipsi alere nos possimus? Quamdiu sationibus implebimus magnarum urbium campos? Quamdiu nobis populus metet? Quamdiu unius mensae instrumentum multa navigia et quidem non ex uno mari subvehent? Taurus paucissimorum iugerum pascuo impletur; una silva elephantis pluribus sufficit; homo et terra et mari pascitur. Quid ergo? Tam insatiabilem nobis natura alvum dedit, cum tam modica corpora dedisset, ut vastissimorum edacissimorumque animalium aviditatem vinceremus? Minime. Quantulum est enim quod naturae datur! Parvo illa dimittitur.

Seneca, to his friend Lucilius, greetings:[1]

I'm lodging a complaint. I'm filing a lawsuit. I am furious! Are you still choosing, even now, what your wet-nurse, babysitter, or mother chose for you? Do you not yet understand how bad their choices have been? So much harm our family's prayers cause us! In fact, they're more harmful the happier their outcome.[2] I am no longer surprised that every kind of awfulness pursues us, beginning from childhood: we grow up amid the accursed prayers of our parents.[3] Let the gods hear us in our *own* voice, on our *own* behalf, with no strings attached.

How long will we beseech the gods for things as if we were not yet able to take care of ourselves? How long will we flood the markets of great cities with grain? How long must the masses bring in the harvest for our sakes? How long must many ships, arriving not from just one sea, convey the accoutrements for a single meal? A bull is sated on a pasture of the fewest acres. One forest is enough for a great many elephants. The human being feeds on land *and* sea. And why is that? Has Nature given us a paunch so insatiable, despite her gift of moderately sized bodies, that we outstrip in greediness the biggest, most voracious animals?

Non fames nobis ventris nostri magno constat, sed ambitio. Hos itaque, ut ait Sallustius, 'ventri oboedientes,' animalium loco numeremus, non hominum, quosdam vero ne animalium quidem, sed mortuorum. Vivit is qui multis usui est; vivit is qui se utitur. Qui vero latitant et torpent sic in domo sunt quomodo in conditivo. Horum licet in limine ipso nomen marmori inscribas: MORTEM SUAM ANTECESSERUNT. VALE.

Hardly. How little it is that our nature requires. Its needs are met with but a morsel. It's not the hunger of our bellies that costs us so much. It's overreach. Those people who, as Sallust puts it,[4] "obey their stomachs" let us count among the animals, not among humankind. In fact, certain people we should count not even among animals— "living beings"—but among the dead. That person who is useful to many is alive. That person is alive who makes use of himself. There are some people, as you know, who hide away and languish at home as if buried in a tomb. You might as well carve this inscription on their marble foyers: DEAD BEFORE THEY DIED. Farewell.

7. Lions, and Tigers, and Bears (Selections from [Aristotle], "On Marvelous Things Heard")

This work, passed down with Aristotle's corpus but certainly not by him, contains fascinating notebook-style accounts of observed and reported behaviors of animals from the Mediterranean region and beyond. The reader may decide for him- or herself what is plausible, what is not, and what is simply outlandish. The translator has given his own verdicts in the notes. Dorothy, the Tin Man, the Scarecrow, and Toto, at any rate, have nothing to fear on that score.

Close observation of animals' agency, sentience, and extraordinary powers surely played a large role in humans deifying nonhuman animals at the dawn of our own emergence as a species. Animals, on this view, were the first gods. That they exude the numinous energy of Life is plain for all to see. As with Aelian in selection 5, it is hard not to come

HOW TO CARE ABOUT ANIMALS

1. Ἐν τῇ Παιονίᾳ φασὶν ἐν τῷ ὄρει τῷ Ἡσαίνῳ κα-
λουμένῳ, ὃ τὴν Παιονικὴν καὶ τὴν Μαιδικὴν ὁρίζει,
εἶναί τι θηρίον τὸ καλούμενον βόλινθον, ὑπὸ δὲ τῶν
Παιόνων μόναιπον. τοῦτον λέγουσι τὴν μὲν ὅλην
φύσιν παραπλήσιον εἶναι βοΐ, διαφέρειν δὲ τῷ με-
γέθει καὶ τῇ εὐρωστίᾳ, προσέτι δὲ καὶ τῇ χαίτῃ· ἔχει
γὰρ ἀπὸ τοῦ αὐχένος, ὥσπερ ὁ ἵππος, κατατείνου-
σαν βαθεῖαν σφόδρα, καὶ ἀπὸ τῆς κορυφῆς ἕως
τῶν ὀφθαλμῶν. τὰ δὲ κέρατα οὐχ ὥσπερ οἱ βόες,
ἀλλὰ κατεστραμμένα, καὶ τὸ ὀξὺ κάτω παρὰ τὰ
ὦτα· χωρεῖν δὲ αὐτὰ ἡμιχόου πλεῖον ἑκάτερον
αὐτῶν, καὶ μέλανα σφόδρα εἶναι, διαστίλβειν δὲ
ὡσανεὶ λελεπισμένα. ὅταν δὲ ἐκδαρῇ τὸ δέρμα,
κατέχειν τόπον ὀκτακλίνου. ἡνίκα δὲ πληγῇ, φεύγει, κἂν ἐξαδυνατοῦν μένει. ἔστι δὲ ἡδύκρεως.
ἀμύνεται δὲ λακτίζον καὶ προσαφοδεῦον ὡς ἐπὶ
τέτταρας ὀργυιάς· ῥᾳδίως δὲ χρῆται τούτῳ καὶ
πολλάκις τῷ εἴδει, καὶ ἐπικαίει δ᾽ ὥστ᾽ ἀποψήχε-
σθαι τὰς τρίχας τῶν κυνῶν. τεταραγμένου μὲν οὖν
τοῦτο ποιεῖν φασι τὸν ἄφοδον, ἀταράχου δὲ μὴ

away feeling some similar awe—albeit mixed with bemusement—from reading these quaint reports.

1. They say that in Paeonia,[1] on the mountain called Hesaenus, which forms the border between Paeonia and Maedice, there is an animal called the *bolinthus*, which the Paeonians call *monaepus*. They say that this animal resembles in its general nature an ox, but it's bigger, stronger, and shaggier. For it has a mane on its neck, like a horse, thick and stretching down from its head to its eyes. Its horns, however, are not like those of oxen but point down to form sharp tips beside the ears. Each of them would hold more than half a pitcher of liquid each. The horns are a deep black but gleam as if they had been peeled. When its hide is skinned, it covers the space of eight couches. When the animal is struck, it flees, and even if it's been disabled it carries on. Its flesh tastes sweet. It protects itself by kicking and by defecating jets of excrement that reach over forty feet. It makes frequent and ready use of this form of defense, which burns so fiercely that it will cause a dog's fur to rub off. They say that the animal does this when it's agitated, but that the dung doesn't burn

ἐπικαίειν. ὅταν δὲ τίκτωσι, πλείους γενόμενοι καὶ συναχθέντες ἅμα πάντες οἱ μέγιστοι τίκτουσι καὶ κύκλῳ προσαφοδεύουσι· πολὺ γάρ τι τούτου τοῦ περιττώματος τὸ θηρίον προΐεται.

30. Ἐν δὲ Σκύθαις τοῖς καλουμένοις Γελωνοῖς φασὶ θηρίον τι γίνεσθαι, σπάνιον μὲν ὑπερβολῇ, ὃ ὀνομάζεται τάρανδος· λέγεται δὲ τοῦτο μεταβάλλειν τὰς χρόας τῆς τριχὸς καθ᾽ ὃν ἂν καὶ τόπον ᾖ. διὰ δὲ τοῦτο εἶναι δυσθήρατον [καὶ διὰ τὴν μεταβολήν] καὶ γὰρ δένδρεσι καὶ τόποις, καὶ ὅλως ἐν οἷς ἂν ᾖ, τοιοῦτον τῇ χροίᾳ γίνεσθαι. θαυμασιώτατον δὲ τὸ τὴν τρίχα μεταβάλλειν· τὰ γὰρ λοιπὰ τὸν χρῶτα, οἷον ὅ τε χαμαιλέων καὶ ὁ πολύπους. τὸ δὲ μέγεθος ὡσανεὶ βοῦς. τοῦ δὲ προσώπου τὸν τύπον ὅμοιον ἔχει ἐλάφῳ.

144. Ἐν Μυσίᾳ φασὶν ἄρκτων τι γένος εἶναι λευκόν, αἳ ὅταν κυνηγῶνται, ἀφιᾶσι τοιαύτην πνοὴν ὥστε τῶν κυνῶν τὰς σάρκας σήπειν, ὡσαύτως δὲ καὶ τῶν λοιπῶν θηρίων, ἀβρώτους τε ποιεῖν. ἐὰν δέ τις καὶ βιάσηται καὶ ἐγγίσῃ, ἀφιᾶσιν ἐκ τοῦ στόματος φλέγμα πάμπολύ τι, ὡς ἔοικεν, ὃ προσφυσᾷ πρὸς τὰ πρόσωπα τῶν κυνῶν, ὡσαύτως δὲ καὶ τῶν ἀνθρώπων, ὥστε καὶ ἀποπνίγειν καὶ ἀποτυφλοῦν.

when the animal feels relaxed. When they give birth, they gather in great numbers as a herd. All the biggest animals deliver their offspring and defecate in a circle. Indeed, the manure this animal generates is more than most.[2]

30. Among the Scythians, who are called the Geloni,[3] they say there is an extremely rare animal called a *tarandos*. It is said to change the color of its hair according to the place where it is. Consequently, it's difficult to hunt because it turns the color of the trees and general locations it finds itself in. The fact that it's a change of hair color is the most amazing thing. Other animals change their skin, like the chameleon and the octopus, but this animal is the size of an ox. And yet its face bears a similar stamp to a deer.[4]

144. In Mysia[5] they say that there is a species of white bear that, when she's hunted, releases such a stench of breath that it causes dogs' flesh to rot. It has the same effect on other animals, too, rendering them inedible. If someone presses on this bear with force and up close, she releases a wad of phlegm from her mouth, so it seems, which sprays into the faces of dogs and human hunters both, choking and blinding them.[6]

145. Ἐν δὲ τῇ Ἀραβίᾳ ὑαινῶν τι γένος φασὶν εἶναι, ὃ ἐπειδὰν προΐδῃ τι θηρίον ἢ ἀνθρώπου ἐπιβῇ ἐπὶ τὴν σκιάν, ἀφωνίαν ἐργάζεται καὶ πῆξιν τοιαύτην ὥστε μὴ δύνασθαι κινεῖν τὸ σῶμα. τοῦτο δὲ ποιεῖν καὶ ἐπὶ τῶν κυνῶν.

7. Ἐν Αἰγύπτῳ δὲ τοὺς τροχίλους φασὶν εἰσπετομένους εἰς τὰ στόματα τῶν κροκοδείλων καθαίρειν αὐτῶν τοὺς ὀδόντας, τὰ σαρκία τὰ ἐνεχόμενα τοῖς ῥύγχεσιν ἐξέλκοντας· τοὺς δ᾽ ἥδεσθαι καὶ μηδὲν βλάπτειν αὐτούς.

8. Τοὺς ἐν Βυζαντίῳ φασὶν ἐχίνους αἰσθάνεσθαι ὅτε βόρεια καὶ νότια πνεῖ πνεύματα, καὶ μεταβάλλειν εὐθὺς τὰς ὀπάς, καὶ ὅταν μὲν ᾖ νότια, ἐκ τοῦ ἐδάφους τὰς ὀπὰς ποιεῖσθαι, ὅταν δὲ βόρεια, ἐκ τῶν τοιχῶν.

10. Φασὶν ἐν Συρίᾳ τῶν ἀγρίων ὄνων ἕνα ἀφηγεῖσθαι τῆς ἀγέλης, ἐπειδὰν δέ τις νεώτερος ὢν τῶν πώλων ἐπί τινα θήλειαν ἀναβῇ, τὸν ἀφηγούμενον θυμοῦσθαι, καὶ διώκειν ἕως τούτου ἕως ἂν καταλάβῃ τὸν πῶλον, καὶ ὑποκύψας ἐπὶ τὰ ὀπίσθια σκέλη τῷ στόματι ἀποσπάσῃ τὰ αἰδοῖα.

12. Τὸ τῆς ἰκτίδος λέγεται αἰδοῖον εἶναι οὐχ ὅμοιον τῇ φύσει τῶν λοιπῶν ζῴων, ἀλλὰ στερεὸν

145. In Arabia they say there is a kind of hyena that, when it sees an animal from afar or crosses the shadow of a human being, it produces muteness in them and such a shock that they cannot move their bodies.[7]

7. They say that in Egypt sandpipers fly into the mouths of crocodiles and clean their teeth for them, picking out bits of flesh that get lodged there using their beaks. The crocodiles enjoy this and do the birds no harm.[8]

8. They say that the hedgehogs in Byzantium perceive when the wind blows from the north or from the south and that they immediately change the configuration of their holes accordingly: when it blows from the south, they dig their holes from underneath and when from the north, they dig through the sides.

10. They say that in Syria a single wild ass is the leader of the pack. When one of the younger foals tries to mount a female, the leader becomes angry, chases after the foal till he catches him, then, lowering his head between his hind legs, bites off his penis.[9]

12. The marten's penis is said to be unlike those of other animals. It is hard like bone all the time,

διὰ παντὸς οἷον ὀστοῦν, ὅπως ἄν ποτε διακειμένη τύχῃ. φασὶ δὲ στραγγουρίας αὐτὸ φάρμακον εἶναι ἐν τοῖς ἀρίστοις, καὶ δίδοσθαι ἐπιξυόμενον.

13. Τὸν δρυοκολάπτην φασὶ τὸ ὄρνεον ἐπὶ τῶν δένδρων βαδίζειν ὥσπερ τοὺς ἀσκαλαβώτας, καὶ ὕπτιον καὶ ἐπὶ τὴν γαστέρα. νέμεσθαι δὲ λέγεται καὶ τοὺς ἐκ τῶν δένδρων σκώληκας, καὶ οὕτω σφόδρα κατὰ βάθους ὀρύττειν τὰ δένδρα ζητοῦντα τοὺς σκώληκας ὥστε καὶ καταβάλλειν αὐτά.

23. Περὶ Θετταλίαν μνημονεύουσιν ὄφεις ζῳογονηθῆναι τοσούτους ὥστε, εἰ μὴ ὑπὸ τῶν πελαργῶν ἀνῃροῦντο, ἐκχωρῆσαι ἂν αὐτούς. διὸ δὴ καὶ τιμῶσι τοὺς πελαργούς, καὶ κτείνειν οὐ νόμος· καὶ ἐάν τις κτείνῃ, ἔνοχος τοῖς αὐτοῖς γίνεται οἷσπερ καὶ ὁ ἀνδροφόνος.

28. Ἐν Κυρήνῃ δέ φασιν οὐχ ἓν εἶναι μυῶν γένος, ἀλλὰ πλείω καὶ διάφορα καὶ ταῖς μορφαῖς καὶ ταῖς χρόαις· ἐνίους γὰρ πλατυπροσώπους, ὥσπερ αἱ γαλαῖ, γίνεσθαι, τινὰς δὲ ἐχινώδεις, οὓς καλοῦσιν ἐχίνας.

70. Φασὶ δὲ καὶ ἐν Σερίφῳ τοὺς βατράχους οὐκ ᾄδειν· ἐὰν δὲ εἰς ἄλλον τόπον μετενεχθῶσιν, ᾄδουσιν.

146. Κατὰ δὲ Συρίαν εἶναί τί φασι ζῷον ὃ καλεῖται λεοντοφόνον· ἀποθνήσκει γὰρ ὁ λέων, ὡς

no matter its state of excitement. They say it is among the best drugs to cure urinary ailments and is administered as a powder.[10]

13. They say that the woodpecker climbs up trees like a lizard upside down on its belly. It is said to feed on grubs in the trees and bores so deeply into them in search of grubs that it actually topples them down.[11]

23. In the region of Thessaly there's mention made of snakes born alive in such quantities that if they weren't eaten by storks the people would move away. Thus, they honor storks, and it is unlawful to kill them. If anyone does kill a stork, he is liable for the same punishments as a murderer.[12]

28. In Cyrene they say that there is not just one kind of mouse, but many, of different shapes and colors. Some are born flatheaded like weasels, but others look like hedgehogs, so they call them hedgehogs.[13]

70. They say that on Seriphus the frogs do not croak, but if they are moved to another place they do.[14]

146. In the region of Syria they say there is a certain animal that is called the lion killer. A lion

ἔοικεν, ὅταν αὐτοῦ φάγῃ. ἑκὼν μὲν οὖν τοῦτο οὐ ποιεῖ, ἀλλὰ φεύγει τὸ ζῷον· ὅταν δὲ συλλαβόντες αὐτὸ οἱ κυνηγέται καὶ ὀπτήσαντες ὥσπερ ἄλφιτα λευκὰ περιπάσσωσιν ἄλλῳ ζῴῳ, γευσάμενοι[1] ἀπόλλυσθαί φασι παραχρῆμα. κακοῖ καὶ προσουροῦν τὸν λέοντα τοῦτο τὸ ζῷον.

165. Τοῦ περκνοῦ ἔχεως τῇ ἐχίδνῃ συγγινομένου, ἡ ἔχιδνα ἐν τῇ συνουσίᾳ τὴν κεφαλὴν ἀποκόπτει. διὰ τοῦτο καὶ τὰ τέκνα, ὥσπερ τὸν θάνατον τοῦ πατρὸς μετερχόμενα, τὴν γαστέρα τῆς μητρὸς διαρρήγνυσιν.

77. Φασὶ δὲ καὶ τὴν φώκην ἐξεμεῖν τὴν πυτίαν, ὅταν ἁλίσκηται· εἶναι δὲ φαρμακῶδες καὶ τοῖς ἐπιλήπτοις χρήσιμον.

dies, apparently, whenever he eats some of this animal. He does not do so on purpose. In fact, he avoids the creature. Hunters, too, when they catch the animal and roast it, sprinkling barley meal on top as one does for other animals, if they take a taste, they are said to die instantly. This animal can harm a lion just by urinating on it.[15]

165. When the male adder mates with a female, the female bites off his head during intercourse. Because of this, the offspring, as if prosecuting the death of their father, burst through the mother's belly.[16]

77. They say the seal vomits rennet when it is caught. This is medicinal and especially useful for epileptics.[17]

8. Quoth the Raven Nevermore (Pliny the Elder, *Natural History* 10.43 and 58–60)

These excerpts come from those books of Pliny's sprawling encyclopedia, the Naturalis Historia *("Inquiries into Nature"), that deal with zoology. Anyone who has seen that David Attenborough segment featuring the Australian lyrebird imitating the sound of a car alarm and of a roaring chainsaw should be prepared to believe everything Pliny says here about the virtuosity of songbirds. There's no doubt that he also anthropomorphizes, as he does in his discussion of elephants (see selection no. 10). But Pliny's genuine admiration for birds is unmistakable, making him a strong contender for being the ancient equivalent of a John James Audubon, working in the medium of words.*

XLIII. Luscinis diebus ac noctibus continuis xv garrulus sine intermissu cantus densante se frondium germine, non in novissimis digna miratu ave. primum tanta vox tam parvo in corpusculo, tam pertinax spiritus; deinde in una perfecta musicae scientia: modulatus editur sonus, et nunc continuo spiritu trahitur in longum, nunc variatur inflexo, nunc distinguitur conciso, copulatur intorto, promittitur revocato; infuscatur ex inopinato, interdum et secum ipse murmurat, plenus, gravis, acutus, creber, extentus, ubi visum est vibrans—summus, medius, imus; breviterque omnia tam parvulis in faucibus quae tot exquisitis tibiarum tormentis ars hominum excogitavit, ut non sit dubium hanc suavitatem praemonstratam efficaci auspicio cum in ore Stesichori cecinit infantis.

ac ne quis dubitet artis esse, plures singulis sunt cantus, nec iidem omnibus, sed sui cuique. certant inter se, palamque animosa contentio est; victa morte finit saepe vitam, spiritu prius deficiente quam cantu. meditantur aliae iuveniores versusque

When the leaves are full in bloom, for fifteen days and nights on end, without a break, the nightingale chirps its chattering song. It is a bird not least in rank, and worthy of admiration. First, what a big voice in so tiny a body! What tenacious puffs of breath! And then what a complete knowledge of music in just one bird! The sound it pours forth is modulated—now drawn out at length with a sustained breath, now varied by bending it, now punctuated by cutting it short, then joined by twisting till given full rein after having been recalled. Then, unexpectedly, the sound darkens, to almost a whisper. The sound can be full; deep; shrill; staccato; expansive; tremulous, when this seems right; soprano; mezzo; baritone—in short, every human skill devised for that exquisite trilling instrument, the flute, resides in such a tiny throat! There can be no doubt that this was the sweetness presaged by that powerful omen of a nightingale perching on the lips of Stesichorus to sing when he was just a babe.[1]

And, so that no one doubt that their skill is an artform, individual birds possess several songs, and not all the same songs, but rather each has its own. They compete with one another, too, and their rivalry is vehement and plain for all to see.

quos imitentur accipiunt; audit discipula intenti-
one magna et reddit, vicibusque reticent; intellegitur emendatae correctio et in docente quaedam
reprehensio. ergo servorum illis pretia sunt, et
quidem ampliora quam quibus olim armigeri
parabantur. scio HS. vi candidam alioquin, quod
est prope invisitatum,[1] venisse quae Agrippinae
Claudii principis coniugi dono daretur. . . .

LVIII. Super omnia humanas voces reddunt,
psittaci quidem etiam sermocinantes. India hanc
avem mittit, siptacen vocat, viridem toto corpore,
torque tantum miniato in cervice distinctam. imperatores salutat et quae accipit verba pronuntiat,
in vino praecipue lasciva. capiti eius duritia eadem
quae rostro; hoc, cum loqui discit, ferreo verbera-
tur radio: non sentit aliter ictus. cum devolat,
rostro se excipit, illi innititur levioremque ita se
pedum infirmitati facit.

QUOTH THE RAVEN NEVERMORE

A losing bird often ends her[2] life by death, her breath failing before her song. Other younger birds practice singing and are given songs to imitate. The pupil listens attentively and repeats back. Student and teacher fall quiet by turns. One can discern improvement in a bird that is corrected, and a kind of critique is offered by the one teaching. And so, these birds fetch prices one pays for slaves. Indeed, larger outlays are paid for them than were paid for arms bearers in the old days. I know of one bird—granted, an albino—that sold for six hundred thousand sesterces, an almost unprecedented sum, which was gifted to Agrippina, the wife of the emperor Claudius. . . .

More than anything, though, birds repeat human voices. Parrots, in fact, even hold forth in conversation. India sends us this bird.[3] Its whole body is green, except for a red-tinged ring around its neck. It salutes its generals[4] and repeats the words it hears—especially lewd talk over wine. Its head is as hard as its beak. Thus, when it's being trained to speak, it's smacked on the head with an iron rod (otherwise, it doesn't feel the blows). When it alights from flying, it catches itself with its beak and leans on it to make itself lighter since its feet are weak.

LIX. Minor nobilitas, quia non ex longinquo venit, sed expressior loquacitas certo generi picarum est. adamant verba quae loquantur nec discunt tantum sed diligunt, meditantesque intra semet cura atque cogitatione intentionem non occultant. constat emori victas difficultate verbi ac, nisi subinde eadem audiant, memoria falli, quaerentesque mirum in modum hilarari si interim audierint id verbum. . . .

Agrippina Claudii Caesaris turdum habuit, quod numquam ante, imitantem sermones hominum. cum haec proderem, habebant et Caesares iuvenes sturnum, item luscinias, Graeco ac Latino sermone dociles, praeterea meditantes assidue et in diem nova loquentes, loquentes, longiore etiam contextu. docentur secreto et ubi nulla alia vox misceatur, adsidente qui crebro dicat ea quae condita velit ac cibis blandiente.

LX. Reddatur et corvis sua gratia, indignatione quoque populi Romani testata, non solum

There is a certain kind of magpie that enjoys less distinction because it does not come from afar, but whose capacity for speech is more expressive. These birds become fond of the words they speak. They don't just learn them, they love them, contemplate them inwardly with careful reflection, and don't make a secret of their efforts. Authorities agree that if they are defeated by the difficulty of a word, they up and die, and that, unless they hear the same words repeated again and again, their memory fails them, but, when searching for a word, they cheer up wonderfully if in the meanwhile they hear that word spoken.

Claudius Caesar's wife, Agrippina, had a thrush that imitated human conversation, which had never been seen before. When I was publishing these reports, the young Caesars[5] had a starling, some nightingales, too, that had been trained to speak Greek and Latin. What is more, they practiced diligently and spoke new phrases every day and in more extended syntax. Birds are taught in private, where no other voice is intermixed. The trainer sits next to the bird, repeating the words he wants it to retain and enticing it with food.

Let's also give ravens the appreciation they're due. One raven's worth was attested by the Roman

conscientia. Tiberio principe ex fetu supra Castorum aedem genito pullus in adpositam sutrinam devolavit, etiam religione commendatus officinae domino. is mature sermoni adsuefactus, omnibus matutinis evolans in rostra in forum versus Tiberium, dein Germanicum et Drusum Caesares nominatim, mox transeuntem populum Romanum salutabat, postea ad tabernam remeans, plurium annorum adsiduo officio mirus. hunc sive aemulatione vicinitatis manceps proximae sutrinae sive iracundia subita, ut voluit videri, excrementis aspersa calceis macula, exanimavit tanta plebei consternatione ut primo pulsus ex ea regione, mox et interemptus sit, funusque aliti innumeris celebratum exequiis, constratum lectum super Aethiopum duorum umeros praecedente tibicine et coronis omnium generum ad rogum usque qui constructus dextra viae Appiae ad secundum lapidem in campo Rediculi appellato fuit. adeo satis iusta causa populo Romano visa est exequiarum ingenium avis ac supplicii de cive Romano in ea urbe in qua multorum principum nemo deduxerat funus, Scipionis vero Aemiliani post Carthaginem Numantiamque deletas ab eo nemo vindicaverat mortem. hoc gestum M. Servilio C. Cestio coss. a. d. v kal. Apriles. . . .

People's indignation, not just by their acknowl-
edgment of its value. When Tiberius was emperor, a raven fledgling that was hatched from a
clutch of eggs laid atop the temple of Castor and
Pollux flew down into a cobbler's shop nearby,
whereafter the proprietor of the shop considered
the bird sacrosanct on account of religion. In time,
the raven took to talking and flew off to the
Forum every morning to greet Tiberius by name
at the Rostrum, then the Caesars Germanicus and
Drusus,[6] and soon the Roman People as they
passed by before he returned to the shop. The bird
performed this duty faithfully for several years
and became a mascot yet was killed by the owner
of the cobbler shop next door, perhaps out of rivalry in the neighborhood, or from a sudden out-
burst of anger (as he wanted it to seem) because
bird droppings had bespattered his stock of shoes.
The raven's death caused such a public outcry that
the cobbler was driven out of the district at first,
and soon thereafter done away with, whereas the
bird got a public funeral attended by a massive
procession of followers, its bier draped with a
cloth and lifted onto the shoulders of two Ethio-
pians with a flute player leading the way. There
were wreaths of all kinds strewn as far as to where

adeo satis iusta causa populo Romano visa est exequiarum ingenium avis ac supplicii de cive Romano in ea urbe in qua multorum principum nemo deduxerat funus, Scipionis vero Aemiliani post Carthaginem Numantiamque deletas ab eo nemo vindicaverat mortem. hoc gestum M. Servilio C. Cestio coss. a. d. v kal. Apriles. . . .

the pyre was situated, which was built on the right side of the Appian Way, at the second milestone, at what is called the Field of Rediculus.[7]

That's how sufficient a justification for a funeral the Roman People considered a bird's genius to be—not to mention the punishment of a Roman citizen—in a city where no one had conducted public funerals even for many leading men. No one, for example, had avenged the death of Scipio Aemilianus despite the fact that he had destroyed Carthage and Numantia.[8] The raven's funeral took place on March 28, in the consulship of Marcus Servilius and Gaius Cestius.[9]

9. Pathetic Fallacy
(Ovid, *Metamorphoses* 10.106–44)

The myth of Cyparissus—about a boy who accidentally kills his pet stag, a love gift from Apollo, and is transformed into a weeping cypress tree from grief—is a tragic tale about the potential consequences of "crossing the line" with wild animals. The setting of Ovid's lay intensifies the pathos: The bard Orpheus has just failed in his attempt to retrieve his wife, Eurydice, from the Underworld. He mourns her, strumming his lyre on a bare slope of the Rhodope Mountains in Thrace (modern Bulgaria). This conjures a forest of trees to come provide him comfort with shade, among them the cypress, and with it this story. Orpheus's plaintive tune soon attracts a congregation of wild animals and birds as well. As Ovid portrays it, Nature responds in cosmic sympathy to the grief and loss sometimes involved in interspecies interactions.

Adfuit huic turbae metas imitata cupressus,
nunc arbor, puer ante deo dilectus ab illo,
qui citharam nervis et nervis temperat arcum.
namque sacer nymphis Carthaea tenentibus
    arva
110 ingens cervus erat, lateque patentibus altas
ipse suo capiti praebebat cornibus umbras.
cornua fulgebant auro, demissaque in armos
pendebant tereti gemmata monilia collo.
bulla super frontem parvis argentea loris
115 vincta movebatur; parilesque ex aere nitebant
auribus e geminis circum cava tempora
    bacae;
isque metu vacuus naturalique pavore
deposito celebrare domos mulcendaque colla
quamlibet ignotis manibus praebere solebat.
120 sed tamen ante alios, Ceae pulcherrime
    gentis,
gratus erat, Cyparisse, tibi: tu pabula
    cervum
ad nova, tu liquidi ducebas fontis ad undam,
tu modo texebas varios per cornua flores,
nunc eques in tergo residens huc laetus et
    illuc
125 mollia purpureis frenabas ora capistris.
Aestus erat mediusque dies, solisque vapore

PATHETIC FALLACY

The conical cypress joined this crowd, now a tree, but once a boy, loved by the god in charge of strings, who plucks the bow and lyre.[1]

There was a mighty stag, you see, sacred to the nymphs that haunt the glades around Carthaea.[2] With antlers spreading wide across his head, he provided himself his own abundant shade. His antlers gleamed with gold, and on his shoulders a collar, studded with jewels, hung from his polished neck.[3] A silver amulet, tied in place with slender leather strips, jangled on his forehead.[4] Gleaming from both ears, framed by the cavities around his temples, were pearl-shaped earrings, each of equal size, in bronze.

Free from fear and setting a stag's natural skittishness aside, he used to visit people's houses and let strangers stroke his neck as they pleased. More than by others, though, he was beloved by *you*, Cyparissus, yourself the most handsome lad of Cean stock. *You* led the stag to fresh pastures. *You* led him to the waters of the clean-flowing spring. It was you who would sometimes weave flower garlands for his antlers or sit like a Knight on his back and take delight in riding him this way and that, a purple halter guiding his pliant mouth.

concava litorei fervebant bracchia Cancri:
fessus in herbosa posuit sua corpora terra
cervus et arborea frigus ducebat ab umbra.
130 hunc puer inprudens iaculo Cyparissus acuto
fixit et, ut saevo morientem vulnere vidit,
velle mori statuit. quae non solacia Phoebus
dixit et, ut leviter pro materiaque doleret,
admonuit! gemit ille tamen munusque
    supremum
135 hoc petit a superis, ut tempore lugeat omni.
iamque per inmensos egesto sanguine fletus
in viridem verti coeperunt membra colorem,
et, modo qui nivea pendebant fronte capilli,
horrida caesaries fieri sumptoque rigore
140 sidereum gracili spectare cacumine caelum.
ingemuit tristisque deus "lugebere nobis
lugebisque alios aderisque dolentibus"
    inquit.
Tale nemus vates attraxerat inque ferarum
concilio, medius turbae, volucrumque
    sedebat.

PATHETIC FALLACY

It was a summer afternoon. The Sun was in Cancer,[5] such that the shore crab's curved claws were scorching the day with a humid haze. Worn out, the stag lay his body down on grassy terrain and began absorbing the coolness of the forest's shade. Unknowingly, the boy Cyparissus pierced him with a sharp javelin, and, as he saw his stag dying from the savage wound, he made up his mind to wish death for himself, too.

What solace did Phoebus[6] not offer then! He urged him to grieve moderately and in a manner that suited the situation. Cyparissus, however, wails on and begs one final gift from the gods above—that he might mourn forever and all time. And now, the boy's lifeblood drained through a flood of tears, his limbs began to change to the color green, and his hair, which hung down from his snow-white brow, became bristly fronds. Then his trunk became stiff, and from his wispy crest he looked out on the starry sky.[7] Apollo groaned, and in sadness said: "You shall be mourned by me. You shall mourn for others. And you will always be where people grieve."[8]

Such was the grove the bard had assembled, and he just sat there, in the middle of the crowd, among a council of wild animals and birds.

10. The Elephant in the Room
(Excerpts from Pliny,
Natural History Book 8)

Pliny the Elder's rich encomium on elephants treats both their celebrated emotional intelligence and the ethically fraught interaction between humans and animals that have been conscripted for service as engines of war and abused for human entertainment. Pliny was a prolific writer, but not a gifted stylist, so takes some coaxing in translation. He is also a bit credulous. But deep respect for animals and, indeed, all of Nature leaps from his page. What he might lack in literary talent (though he can at times be wry and deadpan), he makes up for in tenacity: Pliny died at the foot of Mount Vesuvius while it was erupting in 79 CE, intent on getting a closer look at what was going on.[1] In this respect, he resembles Aristotle's keen scientist (selection no. 1), whose eye is ever trained on the acquisition of greater knowledge and understanding.

Maximum est elephans proximumque humanis
sensibus, quippe intellectus illis sermonis patrii et
imperiorum obedientia, officiorum quae didicere
memoria, amoris et gloriae voluptas, immo vero
quae etiam in homine rara, probitas, prudentia,
aequitas, religio quoque siderum solisque ac lunae
veneratio. auctores sunt in Mauretaniae saltibus
ad quendam amnem cui nomen est Amilo nites-
cente luna nova greges eorum descendere ibique
se purificantes sollemniter aqua circumspergi
atque ita salutato sidere in silvas reverti vitulorum
fatigatos prae se ferentes. alienae quoque religio-
nis intellectu creduntur maria transituri non
ante naves conscendere quam invitati rectoris
iureiurando de reditu. visique sunt fessi aegri-
tudine (quando et illas moles infestant morbi)
herbas supini in caelum iacientes, veluti tellure
precibus allegata. nam quod ad docilitatem at-
tinet regem adorant, genua submittunt, coronas
porrigunt. . . .

THE ELEPHANT IN THE ROOM

The largest land animal, and the one closest to human beings in intelligence, is the elephant. Indeed, the elephant understands the language of its own country, obeys authority, is mindful of the responsibilities it's been taught, and enjoys showing affection and receiving honor.[2] Nay, even more to its credit, it possesses qualities rarely seen even in a human being: probity, good sense, fairness, and religion, too, in its veneration of the sun, moon, and stars. Certain writers state that in the savannahs of Mauretania,[3] when the new moon shines bright, elephant herds go down to a river called the Amilo and sprinkle themselves with water as an act of purification and as a greeting to that heavenly body, whereupon they return to the forest, carrying their tired calves in front of them. They are also believed to possess an understanding of the religion of others, for they will not get on board ship to cross the sea until they are assured by a sworn oath from the captain that they will return.[4] When they are worn down with sickness (since diseases infect even so large a body mass as theirs), they have also been observed to lie on their backs and toss grass up to heaven, as though entreating the Earth with their prayers.

Romae iuncti primum subiere currum Pompei Magni Africano triumpho, quod prius India victa triumphante Libero patre memoratur. . . .

Germanici Caesaris munere gladiatorio quosdam etiam inconditos meatus edidere saltantium modo. vulgare erat per auras arma iacere non auferentibus ventis atque inter se gladiatorios congressus edere aut lascivienti pyrriche conludere. postea et per funes incessere, lecticis etiam ferentes quaterni singulos puerperas imitantes, plenisque homine tricliniis accubitum iere per lectos ita libratis vestigiis ne quis potantium attingeretur.

Mucianus iii consul auctor est aliquem ex his et litterarum ductus Graecarum didicisse solitumque perscribere eius linguae verbis: 'Ipse ego haec scripsi et spolia Celtica dicavi,' itemque se vidente Puteolis, cum advecti e nave egredi

THE ELEPHANT IN THE ROOM

As far as docility goes, they genuflect before a king in adoration, and offer him garlands. . . .

At Rome, elephants were first yoked to pull a chariot in Pompey the Great's African triumph, a practice that is attested, earlier, too, when Father Liber triumphed over India.[5]

At a gladiatorial show put on by Germanicus Caesar elephants performed certain awkward movements in the manner of leaping dancers. It was a popular display for them to throw weapons through the air without the wind blowing them off course and to conduct gladiatorial combats with one another, or to prance about together in a playful Pyrrhic dance.[6] Later on, they would also come to walk along tight ropes, and even— four of them at once—to carry around litters with individuals pretending to be giving birth in them. They would also walk among the couches in a dining room full of people, balancing their steps in such a way that they wouldn't bump into any of the revelers.

Mucianus, three times a consul,[7] has written that one elephant learned the shapes of the Greek letters and was in the habit of writing out in the words of that language: "I myself have written this and have dedicated these spoils taken from

cogerentur, territos spatio pontis procul a conti-
nente porrecti, ut sese longinquitatis aestima-
tione fallerent, aversos retrorsus isse.

IV. Praedam ipsi in se expetendam sciunt solam
esse in armis suis quae Iuba cornua appellat,
Herodotus tanto antiquior et consuetudo melius
dentes; quamobrem deciduos casu aliquo vel senecta defodiunt. hoc solum ebur est: cetero et in
his quoque quae corpus intexit vilitas ossea; qua-
mquam nuper ossa etiam in laminas secari coepere
paenuria, etenim rara amplitudo iam dentium
praeterquam ex India reperitur, cetera in nostro
orbe cessere luxuriae.

dentium candore intellegitur iuventa. circa
hos beluis summa cura: alterius mucroni parcunt
ne sit proeliis hebes, alterius operario usu fodi-
unt radices, inpellunt moles; circumventique a

the Celts." He also says, based on eyewitness testimony, that when elephants were conveyed to Puteoli and were forced to disembark ship, they feared the length of the gangway, which stretched quite a distance from shore, and so they walked backward to fool themselves in their estimation of its length.

Elephants are well aware that the only booty to be had from them resides in their weapons, which Juba calls "horns," but which Herodotus (a much more ancient author) and common custom better describe as "tusks."[8] Accordingly, when one of these falls out because of some accident or from old age, elephants bury them. The tusk alone is of ivory. As for the rest, even among elephants, what other structure the body encases is worthless, comprising only bone. Nonetheless, recently, people have begun to cut elephant bones, too, into layers, on account of a lack of resources, for an abundance of tusks is hard to find, except ones from India, since everything else in our world has fallen prey to luxury.

You can tell an elephant is young by the whiteness of its tusks. The beasts treat their tusks with the greatest care, too. They spare the point of one tusk, for example, so that it will not be blunt for

venantibus primos constituunt quibus sint min-
umi, ne tanti proelium putetur, postea fessi in-
pactos arbori frangunt praedaque se redimunt.

=8.10.31 Dentibus ingens pretium et deorum
simulacris lautissima ex his materia. invenit lux-
uria commendationem et aliam expetiti in callo
manus saporis haut alia de causa, credo, quam
quia ipsum ebur sibi mandere videtur. magnitudo
dentium videtur quidem in templis praecipua, sed
tamen in extremis Africae, qua confinis Aethio-
piae est, postium vicem in domiciliis praebere,
saepesque in his et pecorum stabulis pro palis
elephantorum dentibus fieri Polybius tradidit
auctore Gulusa regulo.

Elephanti gregatim semper ingrediuntur; ducit
agmen maximus natu, cogit aetate proximus.

battles, while they use the other for everyday tasks like digging roots and pushing large objects. When surrounded by hunters, they station those with the smallest tusks in front, so that the hunters think it's not worth the fight. Afterward, if tired out from an attack, they break their tusks by smashing them against a tree, and ransom themselves at the price of the booty they're hunted for.

Tusks cost an enormous amount of money, and they supply the most sumptuous material for images of the gods. But luxury has invented yet another reason for recommending the elephant, namely the flavor of its trunk's hard skin, which is sought out, in my opinion, for no other reason than because the gourmand imagines he's *chewing on ivory*! Although the special prominence of tusks is obvious, given the number of them in temples, in the deepest parts of the province of Africa, on the border with Ethiopia, Polybius reports[9] (on the authority of the chieftain Gulusa) that elephant tusks provide a substitute for doorjambs in houses and are used in the construction of paddocks and stalls for livestock instead of posts.[10] . . .

Elephants always march in a herd. The oldest leads the column and the next eldest brings up the

amnem transituri minimos praemittunt, ne mai-
orum ingressu atterente alveum crescat gurgitis
altitudo. Antipater auctor est duos Antiocho regi
in bellicis usibus celebres etiam cognominibus
fuisse; etenim novere ea. certe Cato, cum inpera-
torum nomina annalibus detraxerit, elephantum
qui fortissime proeliatus esset in Punica acie
Syrum tradidit vocatum altero dente mutilato.
Antiocho vadum fluminis experienti renuit Aiax,
alioqui dux agminis semper; tum pronuntiatum
eius fore pricipatum qui transisset, ausumque Pa-
troclum ob id phaleris argenteis, quo maxime
gaudent, et reliquo omni primatu donavit. ille qui
notabatur inedia mortem ignominiae praetulit;
mirus namque pudor est, victusque vocem fugit
victoris, terram ac verbenas porrigit.

rear. When faced with crossing a river they put the smallest elephants up front to prevent the depth of the flow from increasing by the bigger elephants wearing a deep track in the river's bottom by their walking. Antipater[11] writes that two elephants enlisted by King Antiochus were the talk of the town, known even by name. In fact, elephants know their own names. And, of course, there's Cato, who, although he has deleted the names of generals from his *Annals*,[12] nevertheless recorded that the elephant who was deemed the bravest warrior in the Carthaginian front line was called Syrus, and that he had a broken tusk. When Antiochus was trying to ford a river, his elephant Ajax refused, even though he had always been the leader of the column. Antiochus then made a public announcement that if any elephant would cross the river, he would become commander-in-chief. Whereupon one Patroclus took up the challenge. Accordingly, Antiochus gifted him a silver harness, which delighted Patroclus to no end, and conferred on him every other mark of rank that remained. Ajax, meanwhile, was reprimanded and preferred death by starvation to humiliation, for an elephant's sense of shame is remarkable: an elephant who has been defeated avoids the sound

pudore numquam nisi in abdito coeunt . . . nec
adulteria novere, nullave propter feminas inter se
proelia ceteris animalibus pernicialia, nec quia desit
illis amoris vis, namque traditur unus amasse quandam in Aegypto corallas vendentem ac (ne quis
volgariter electam putet) mire gratam Aristophani
celeberrimo in arte grammatica, alius Menandrum
Syracusanum incipientis iuventae in exercitu Ptolo-
maei, desiderium eius, quotiens non videret, inedia
testatus. et unguentariam quandam dilectam Iuba
tradit. omnium amoris fuere argumenta gaudium
ad conspectum blanditiaeque inconditae, stipesque
quas populus dedisset servatae et in sinum effusae.
nec mirum esse amorem quibus sit memoria. idem
namque tradit agnitum in senecta multos post
annos qui rector in iuventa fuisset; idem divinatio-
nem quandam iustitiae, cum Bocchus rex triginta
elephantis totidem in quos saevire instituerat stipi-
tibus adligatos obiecisset, procursantibus inter eos
qui lacesserent, nec[1] potuisse effici ut crudelitatis
alienae ministerio fungerentur. . . .

of his conqueror's voice and offers earth and branches in supplication.

Because they are modest, elephants never mate except in private. . . . They have no concept of adultery; nor do they fight among themselves over females, which proves so deadly among other animal species. But that is not because they lack the capacity for love. For it is reported that one elephant in Egypt fell in love with a certain girl, a flower seller, who was (lest anyone think the elephant was indiscriminate in choosing her) the special favorite of Aristophanes, a very famous scholar.[13] Another elephant is said to have fallen in love with one Menander of Syracuse, a young soldier in Ptolemy's army. Whenever this elephant did not see his beloved, he gave proof of his longing by refusing to eat. Juba, too, writes about a certain perfume seller who was loved by an elephant. The evidence of their love in every instance was the joy these elephants expressed at the sight of their loved ones, their clumsy flirting, and the fact that they would hold onto the fronds people fed them and lay them lavishly on their loved ones' laps. And it's no wonder animals that possess memory also feel love. For example, Juba also reports how an elephant in old age recognized a

VII. . . . Pompei quoque altero consulatu, dedicatione templi Veneris Victricis, viginti pugnavere in circo aut, ut quidam tradunt, xvii, Gaetulis ex adverso iaculantibus, mirabili unius dimicatione, qui pedibus confossis repsit genibus in catervas, abrepta scuta iaciens in sublime, quae decidentia voluptati spectantibus erant in orbem circumacta, velut arte non furore beluae iacerentur. magnum et in altero miraculum fuit uno ictu occiso; pilum etenim sub oculo adactum in vitalia capitis venerat. universi eruptionem temptavere, non sine vexatione populi, circumdatis claustris ferreis. . . . sed Pompeiani missa fugae spe misericordiam vulgi inenarrabili habitu quaerentes supplicavere quadam sese lamentatione conplorantes, tanto

man who had been his trainer as a youth. He notes this instance, too, which suggests that elephants might possess a sense of justice: when King Bocchus[14] tied thirty elephants to stakes to condemn them to death,[15] then ordered thirty other elephants to savage them as men ran about inciting those elephants to attack, it proved impossible to get them to perform the task of aiding and abetting someone else in his cruelty. . . .

During Pompey's second consulship, at the dedication of the temple to Venus Victrix, twenty elephants (some say seventeen) fought in the Circus. Their opponents were Gaetulians armed with javelins. One of the elephants put up an amazing fight: his feet were destroyed so he crawled on his knees against the Gaetulian throng, snatching away their shields and flinging them into the air. The curved trajectories made by the shields as they fell to the ground delighted the spectators— as if they were being tossed artistically and not merely hurled by an angry behemoth. The audience was also mightily impressed when another elephant was killed by a single blow, for a javelin struck it just below its eye and the weapon had penetrated to the vital parts of the head. At that, *all* the elephants present tried to break out of the

populi dolore ut oblitus imperatoris ac munifi-
centiae honori suo exquisitae flens universus
consurgeret dirasque Pompeio quas ille mox luit
inprecaretur. . . .

Ipsius animalis tanta narratur clementia contra
minus validos ut in grege pecudum occurrentia
manu dimoveat, ne quod obterat inprudens. nec
nisi lacessiti nocent.

iron gates that constrained them, which caused a general panic. . . . However, when Pompey's elephants had lost all hope of escape, they sought mercy from the crowd and entreated it with gestures no words can describe, bemoaning their fate with a kind of wailing. The People were so upset to see this that they forgot all about the general and his lavish munificence in their honor, but arose as a body, tears in their eyes, and called down dire curses on Pompey, who soon afterward paid the price for them.[16]

The gentleness of this animal toward those creatures that are weaker is reported to be so great that if a flock of sheep crosses an elephant's path, it moves them out of the way with its trunk so as not to stomp on any of the sheep unintentionally. In fact, elephants do no harm unless provoked.

11. Pigs Is Equal (Plutarch, *Gryllus*, from the *Moralia* [985d–992e], Abridged)

This disquisition,[1] humorously cast as an interview between Odysseus and Circe based on events described in Odyssey *book 10, indicts the Homeric hero's human failings while extolling the superiority of animals. Circe introduces Odysseus to one of the men in her menagerie whom she has turned into a pig. Plutarch uses the comedic setting to air various arguments for animal excellence, some of them a tad specious, others more serious. Offered transformation back into human form, Gryllus ("Oinker") says no thanks! The sentiment that informs this rhetorical and philosophical exercise is reminiscent of that adage of old folklore, sometimes attributed to Winston Churchill: "Cats look down on you; dogs look up to you; but pigs is equal."*

HOW TO CARE ABOUT ANIMALS

1. ΟΔΥΣΣΕΥΣ
Ταῦτα μέν, ὦ Κίρκη, μεμαθηκέναι δοκῶ καὶ διαμνημονεύσειν· ἡδέως δ᾽ ἄν σου πυθοίμην, εἴ τινας ἔχεις Ἕλληνας ἐν τούτοις, οὓς λύκους καὶ λέοντας ἐξ ἀνθρώπων πεποίηκας.

ΚΙΡΚΗ
Καὶ πολλούς, ὦ ποθούμεν᾽ Ὀδυσσεῦ. πρὸς τί δὲ τοῦτο ἐρωτᾷς;

ΟΔ.
Ὅτι νὴ Δία καλὴν ἄν μοι δοκῶ γενέσθαι φιλοτιμίαν πρὸς τοὺς Ἕλληνας, εἰ χάριτι σῇ λαβὼν τούτους, αὖθις [εἰς] ἀνθρώπους ἑταίρους ἀνασώσαιμι καὶ μὴ περιίδοιμι κατα-γηράσαντας παρὰ φύσιν ἐν σώμασι θηρίων, οἰκτρὰν καὶ ἄτιμον οὕτω δίαιταν ἔχοντας.

ΚΙΡ.
Οὗτος ὁ ἀνὴρ οὐχ αὑτῷ μόνον οὐδὲ τοῖς ἑταίροις, ἀλλὰ τοῖς μηδὲν προσήκουσιν οἴεται δεῖν ὑπ᾽ ἀβελτερίας συμφορὰν γενέσθαι τὴν αὑτοῦ φιλοτιμίαν.

ODYSSEUS

I think I've got it, Circe, and I'll keep all that in mind.[2] I'd be keen to hear from you, though, whether you're keeping any Greeks among those people you've turned into lions and wolves.

CIRCE

Quite a few, Odysseus, sweetheart. Why do you ask?

ODYSSEUS

Because, well, to be honest, I think it would be a great credit to me in the eyes of the Greeks if, with a favor from you, I could rescue my companions—take them home as human beings and not let them grow old unnaturally in the bodies of beasts to live the life they have now, which is pitiful and undignified.

CIRCE

Ha! You vainly think that your own love of honor must become the ruin, not only of yourself and your companions, but even of perfect strangers!

ΟΔ.

Ἕτερον αὖ τινα τοῦτον, ὦ Κίρκη, κυκεῶνα λόγων ταράττεις καὶ ὑποφαρμάττεις, ἐμὲ γοῦν ἀτεχνῶς ποιοῦσα θηρίον, εἰ πείσομαί σοι ὡς συμφορά ἐστιν ἄνθρωπον ἐκ θηρίου γενέσθαι.

ΚΙΡ.

Οὐ γὰρ ἤδη τούτων ἀτοπώτερα πεποίηκας σεαυτόν, ὃς τὸν ἀθάνατον καὶ ἀγήρω σὺν ἐμοὶ βίον ἀφεὶς ἐπὶ γυναῖκα θνητήν, ὡς δ᾽ ἐγώ φημι, καὶ γραῦν ἤδη διὰ μυρίων ἔτι κακῶν σπεύδεις, ὡς δὴ περίβλεπτος ἐκ τούτου καὶ ὀνομαστὸς ἔτι μᾶλλον ἢ νῦν γενόμενος, κενὸν ἀγαθὸν καὶ εἴδωλον ἀντὶ τῆς ἀληθείας διώκων;

ΟΔ.

Ἐχέτω ταῦτα ὡς λέγεις, ὦ Κίρκη· τί γὰρ δεῖ πολλάκις ζυγομαχεῖν ἡμᾶς περὶ τῶν αὐτῶν; τούτους δέ μοι δὸς ἀναλύσασα καὶ χάρισαι τοὺς ἄνδρας.

ΚΙΡ.

Οὐχ οὕτω γ᾽ ἁπλῶς, μὰ τὴν Ἑκάτην· οὐ γὰρ οἱ τυχόντες εἰσίν· ἀλλ᾽ ἐροῦ πρῶτον αὐτούς, εἰ θέλουσιν· ἂν δὲ μὴ φῶσι, διαλεχθείς,

PIGS IS EQUAL

ODYSSEUS
Whoa there, Circe! That's a weird sort of word potion you're churning and charming me with again![3] You'll make an animal out of me yet if I am to believe that to be turned from beastly into human form spells ruin.

CIRCE
Have you not in fact performed stranger magic on yourself already? You refused an ageless and eternal life here with me to hurry back instead via ten thousand tribulations to a mortal woman, who is by now, I guarantee you, old to boot[4]—all to make yourself more admired and renowned than you currently are! You're chasing an empty gain, a phantom, instead of what is truly real.

ODYSSEUS
Suit yourself, Circe. But must we have this lovers' spat over and over, always about the same things? Will you please just do me the favor of setting my men free?

CIRCE
Hecate be my witness,[5] it's not as simple as that. These are not your everyday animals. You'll have to ask them first if that is what

ὦ γενναῖε, πεῖσον· ἐὰν δὲ μὴ πείσῃς, ἀλλὰ
καὶ περιγένωνται διαλεγόμενοι, ἱκανὸν ἔστω
σοι περὶ σεαυτοῦ καὶ τῶν φίλων κακῶς
βεβουλεῦσθαι.

ΟΔ.
Τί μου καταγελᾷς, ὦ μακαρία; πῶς γὰρ ἂν ἢ
δοῖεν οὗτοι λόγον ἢ λάβοιεν, ἕως ὄνοι καὶ
σύες καὶ λέοντές εἰσι;

ΚΙΡ.
Θάρρει, φιλοτιμότατ᾽ ἀνθρώπων· ἐγώ σοι
παρέξω καὶ συνιέντας αὐτοὺς καὶ διαλεγομέ-
νους· μᾶλλον δ᾽ εἷς ἱκανὸς ἔσται καὶ διδοὺς
καὶ λαμβάνων ὑπὲρ πάντων λόγον· ἰδού,
τούτῳ διαλέγου.

ΟΔ.
Καὶ τίνα τοῦτον, ὦ Κίρκη, προσαγορεύσομεν;
ἢ τίς ἦν οὗτος ἀνθρώπων;

ΚΙΡ.
Τί γὰρ τοῦτο πρὸς τὸν λόγον; ἀλλὰ κάλει
αὐτόν, εἰ βούλει, Γρύλλον. ἐγὼ δ᾽ ἐκστήσομαι

they want, and, if they refuse, Your Highness, you'll have to discuss it with them and convince them. If you fail to do so—that is, if they prevail in your discussion—you'll have to settle for having judged poorly about yourself and your friends.

ODYSSEUS
O Blessed Mistress—Are you mocking me? How can they engage in the give and take of argument so long as they're asses, pigs, and lions?

CIRCE
Don't you worry, Mr. Most Vainglorious. I'll make sure that they understand you and that they are conversational. Actually, let's let one of them suffice to engage in the give and take of argument on behalf of all. Here you go—talk to this one!

ODYSSEUS
And who is this one that I will address, Circe? Who in the world was he?[6]

CIRCE
What does *that* have to do with the argument? Call him Gryllus—"Oinker"—if you

ὑμῖν, μὴ καὶ παρὰ γνώμην ἐμοὶ δοκῇ χαριζό-
μενος διαλέγεσθαι.

2. ΓΡΥΛΛΟΣ
Χαῖρε, Ὀδυσσεῦ.

ΟΔ.
Καὶ σὺ νὴ Δία, Γρύλλε.

ΓΡ.
Τί βούλει ἐρωτᾶν;

ΟΔ.
Ἐγὼ γινώσκων ὑμᾶς ἀνθρώπους γεγονότας
οἰκτείρω μὲν ἅπαντας οὕτως ἔχοντας, εἰκὸς
δέ μοι μᾶλλον διαφέρειν ὅσοι Ἕλληνες ὄντες
εἰς ταύτην ἀφῖχθε τὴν δυστυχίαν· νῦν οὖν
ἐποιησάμην τῆς Κίρκης δέησιν ὅπως τὸν
βουλόμενον ὑμῶν ἀναλύσασα καὶ καταστή-
σασα πάλιν εἰς τὸ ἀρχαῖον εἶδος ἀποπέμψῃ
μεθ᾽ ἡμῶν.

ΓΡ.
Παῦε, Ὀδυσσεῦ, καὶ περαιτέρω μηδὲν εἴπῃς·
ὡς καὶ σοῦ πάντες ἡμεῖς καταφρονοῦμεν, ὡς
μάτην ἄρα δεινὸς ἐλέγου καὶ τῷ φρονεῖν πολὺ
τῶν ἄλλων ἀνθρώπων ἐδόκεις διαφέρειν, ὃς

want. But I'll get out of the way of you two
to prevent the appearance that he's speaking
against his own convictions to please me.
(Circe exits stage left.)

GRYLLUS
Hi there, Odysseus.

ODYSSEUS
And hello to you, too, Gryllus. Good God!

GRYLLUS
What is it you wish to ask?

ODYSSEUS
I know you used to be people, and I feel
sorry for all of you, living in this way, but
it'll come as no surprise that those of you
who were once Greeks before you came to
this misfortune matter even more to me. So,
accordingly, I have asked Circe to release
and restore to his former state any man who
wants it and to send him back with me.

GRYLLUS
Stop right there, Odysseus. Say nothing
more! All of *us* despise *you* in your state,
too. All along, we've now realized, you were
said to be clever and were thought to exceed

αὐτὸ τοῦτ᾽ ἔδεισας, τὴν μεταβολὴν ἐκ χει-
ρόνων εἰς ἀμείνω, μὴ σκεψάμενος· ὡς γὰρ οἱ
παῖδες τὰ φάρμακα τῶν ἰατρῶν φοβοῦνται,
καὶ τὰ μαθήματα³ φεύγουσιν, ἃ μεταβάλλο-
ντα ἐκ νοσερῶν καὶ ἀνοήτων ὑγιεινοτέρους
καὶ φρονιμωτέρους ποιοῦσιν αὐτούς, οὕτω
σὺ διεκρούσω τὸ ἄλλος ἐξ ἄλλου γενέσθαι,
καὶ νῦν αὐτός τε φρίττων καὶ ὑποδειμαίνων
τῇ Κίρκῃ σύνει, μή σε ποιήσῃ λαθοῦσα σῦν ἢ
λύκον, ἡμᾶς τε πείθεις, ἐν ἀφθόνοις ζῶντας
ἀγαθοῖς, ἀπολιπόντας ἅμα τούτοις τὴν ταῦτα
παρασκευάζουσαν ἐκπλεῖν μετὰ σοῦ, τὸ πάντων βαρυποτμότατον ζῷον αὖθις ἀνθρώπους γενομένους.

ΟΔ.
Ἐμοὶ σύ, Γρύλλε, δοκεῖς οὐ τὴν μορφὴν μόνον
ἀλλὰ καὶ τὴν διάνοιαν ὑπὸ τοῦ πόματος ἐκείνου διεφθάρθαι καὶ γεγονέναι μεστὸς ἀτό-
πων καὶ διαλελωβημένων παντάπασι δοξῶν·

all other men in intelligence, but these were empty claims. You're afraid of changing from what is worse to what is better,[7] not having considered the matter. Just as children fear the doctors' medicines and avoid their schoolwork—things that promote a change of state from sickness and stupidity and which will make them healthier and to have better judgment—so too you resist transformation from one state to another. Even now, at this moment, you shiver and cringe at Circe's side, fearing that, without warning, she might turn you into a pig or a wolf, while simultaneously trying to persuade us, who are living in an abundance of good things, to leave those things behind, along with the woman who provides them, and, having again become human beings— that most luckless animal of all!—sail off with *you*?

ODYSSEUS
Gryllus, you seem to me to have lost not only your form, but your mind as well under influence of that potion. These are wholly strange and tainted ideas that you have

ἢ σέ τις αὖ συηνίας ἡδονὴ πρὸς τόδε τὸ σῶμα
καταγεγοήτευκεν;

ΓΡ.

Οὐδέτερα τούτων, ὦ βασιλεῦ Κεφαλλήνων·
ἂν δὲ διαλέγεσθαι μᾶλλον ἐθέλῃς ἢ λοιδορεῖ-
σθαι, ταχύ σε μεταπείσομεν, ἑκατέρου τῶν
βίων ἐμπείρως ἔχοντες, ὅτι ταῦτα πρὸ ἐκείνων
εἰκότως ἀγαπῶμεν.

ΟΔ.
Ἀλλὰ μὴν ἐγὼ πρόθυμος ἀκροᾶσθαι.

3. ΓΡ.
Καὶ ἡμεῖς τοίνυν λέγειν. ἀρκτέον δὲ πρῶτον
ἀπὸ τῶν ἀρετῶν, ἐφ᾽ αἷς ὁρῶμεν ὑμᾶς μέγα
φρονοῦντας, ὡς τῶν θηρίων πολὺ καὶ δικαι-
οσύνῃ καὶ φρονήσει καὶ ἀνδρείᾳ καὶ ταῖς ἄλλαις ἀρεταῖς διαφέροντας. ἀπόκριναι δή μοι,
σοφώτατ᾽ ἀνδρῶν· ἤκουσα γάρ σου ποτὲ
διηγουμένου τῇ Κίρκῃ περὶ τῆς τῶν Κυκλώ-
πων γῆς, ὡς οὔτ᾽ ἀρουμένη τὸ παράπαν, οὔτε
τινὸς εἰς αὐτὴν φυτεύοντος οὐδέν, οὕτως
ἐστὶν ἀγαθὴ καὶ γενναία τὴν φύσιν, ὥσθ᾽
ἅπαντας ἐκφέρειν τοὺς καρποὺς ἀφ᾽ αὐτῆς·

become infected with. Or perhaps, rather, you already took a kind of pleasure in swinishness and that conjured you into this body?

GRYLLUS
Neither of these things, king of Cephallenians.[8] But if you're willing to talk it over instead of flinging insults, I will quickly make you agree that, seeing that we are acquainted with both ways of life, it makes sense for us to be content with this one instead of our former one.

ODYSSEUS
Alright, then. I'm keen to hear it.

GRYLLUS
And I, in turn, to tell it. Let's begin with the virtues, which, we observe, you humans[9] take great pride in, since you think you are far superior to animals in justice, good judgment, courage, and the other virtues. But answer me this, cleverest of men: I once heard you telling Circe about the Cyclops's land, how it's not ploughed at all, nor does anyone plant anything in it, yet it is of such natural good quality that it bears every sort of fruit of its own accord.[10]

πότερον οὖν ταύτην ἐπαινεῖς μᾶλλον ἢ τὴν αἰ-
γίβοτον Ἰθάκην καὶ τραχεῖαν, ἢ μόλις ἀπ'
ἔργων τε πολλῶν καὶ διὰ πόνων μεγάλων
μικρὰ καὶ γλίσχρα καὶ μηδενὸς ἄξια τοῖς γε-
ωργοῦσιν ἀναδίδωσι; καὶ ὅπως οὐ χαλεπῶς
οἴσεις, παρὰ τὸ φαινόμενον εὐνοίᾳ τῆς πατρί-
δος ἀποκρινόμενος.

ΟΔ.
Ἀλλ' οὐ δεῖ ψεύδεσθαι· φιλῶ μὲν γὰρ καὶ
ἀσπάζομαι τὴν ἐμαυτοῦ πατρίδα καὶ χώραν
μᾶλλον, ἐπαινῶ δὲ καὶ θαυμάζω τὴν ἐκείνων.

ΓΡ.
Οὐκοῦν τοῦτο μὲν οὕτως ἔχειν φήσομεν, ὡς
ὁ φρονιμώτατος ἀνθρώπων ἄλλα μὲν οἴεται
δεῖν ἐπαινεῖν καὶ δοκιμάζειν ἄλλα δ' αἱρεῖσθαι
καὶ ἀγαπᾶν, ἐκεῖνο δ' οἶμαί σε καὶ περὶ τῆς
ψυχῆς ἀποκεκρίσθαι· ταὐτὸν γάρ ἐστι τῷ περὶ
τῆς χώρας, ὡς ἀμείνων ἥτις ἄνευ πόνου τὴν
ἀρετὴν ὥσπερ αὐτοφυῆ καρπὸν ἀναδίδωσιν.

ΟΔ.
Ἔστω σοι καὶ τοῦθ' οὕτως.

Do you, then, praise this land more than rough, goat-foddering Ithaca,[11] which yields scanty, shabby returns worth nothing to its farmers, and even that obtained only with much work and great toil? See to it that you don't take offense and answer contrary to what is obvious out of partiality for your homeland.

ODYSSEUS
I've no need to speak falsely: while I love and cherish my homeland and country more, I nonetheless praise and marvel at the Cyclops's land.

GRYLLUS
This, then, we shall say is how the argument now stands: The most prudent among men thinks he must praise and approve one thing while choosing and loving another. I infer that that would be your response about the soul as well. For the issue is the same there as with land, namely that whatever soul produces virtue like a self-generating crop without toil is better.

ODYSSEUS
Yes, I'll grant that.

ΓΡ.

Ἤδη δ᾿ οὖν ὁμολογεῖς τὴν τῶν θηρίων ψυχὴν εὐφυεστέραν εἶναι πρὸς γένεσιν ἀρετῆς καὶ τελειοτέραν· ἀνεπίτακτος γὰρ καὶ ἀδίδακτος ὥσπερ ἄσπορος καὶ ἀνήροτος ἐκφέρει καὶ αὔξει κατὰ φύσιν τὴν ἑκάστῳ προσήκουσαν ἀρετήν.

ΟΔ.

Καὶ τίνος ποτ᾿ ἀρετῆς, ὦ Γρύλλε, μέτεστι τοῖς θηρίοις;

4. ΓΡ.

Τίνος μὲν οὖν οὐχὶ μᾶλλον ἢ τῷ σοφωτάτῳ τῶν ἀνθρώπων; σκόπει δὲ πρῶτον, εἰ βούλει, τὴν ἀνδρείαν, ἐφ᾿ ᾗ σὺ φρονεῖς μέγα καὶ οὐκ ἐγκαλύπτῃ "θρασὺς" καὶ "πτολίπορθος" ἀποκαλούμενος, ὅστις, ὦ σχετλιώτατε, δόλοις καὶ μηχαναῖς ἀνθρώπους ἁπλοῦν καὶ γεν- ναῖον εἰδότας πολέμου τρόπον ἀπάτης δὲ καὶ ψευδῶν ἀπείρους παρακρουσάμενος, ὄνομα τῇ πανουργίᾳ προστίθης τῆς ἀρετῆς τῆς ἥκιστα πανουργίαν προσιεμένης. ἀλλὰ τῶν γε θηρίων τοὺς πρὸς ἄλληλα καὶ πρὸς ὑμᾶς ἀγῶνας ὁρᾷς ὡς ἄδολοι καὶ ἄτεχνοι καὶ μετ᾿ ἐμφανοῦς γυμνοῦ τε τοῦ θαρρεῖν πρὸς

PIGS IS EQUAL

GRYLLUS
Well, then, you're already agreeing that the soul of animals is more perfect and more naturally suited for the generation of virtue, for, unbidden and untaught—"unsown and unploughed," as it were[12]—it naturally produces and develops the virtue that is appropriate to each creature.

ODYSSEUS
And what of kind of virtue do animals ever possess, Gryllus?

GRYLLUS
What kind of virtue *don't* they possess to a greater extent than the wisest among humans? Consider, first, if you will, courage. You pride yourself on it and don't even cover your head to demur when you are called "fierce" and "sacker of cities."[13] And yet, most unflinching one,[14] you have corrupted men who are familiar with a straightforward and honest way of war, they themselves innocent of deceit and falsehoods, through your tricks and machinations.[15] By villainy you confer on villainy the name of virtue, which is least compatible

ἀληθινῆς ἀλκῆς ποιοῦνται τὰς ἀμύνας καὶ
οὔτε νόμου καλοῦντος οὔτ᾽ ἀστρατείας δε-
δοικότα γραφὴν ἀλλὰ φύσει φεύγοντα τὸ
κρατεῖσθαι μέχρι τῶν ἐσχάτων ἐγκαρτερεῖ
καὶ διαφυλάττει τὸ ἀήττητον· οὐ γὰρ ἡττᾶται
κρατούμενα τοῖς σώμασιν οὐδ᾽ ἀπαγορεύει
ταῖς ψυχαῖς ἀλλὰ ταῖς μάχαις ἐναποθνήσκει.
πολλῶν δὲ θνησκόντων ἡ ἀλκὴ μετὰ τοῦ
θυμοειδοῦς ἀποχωρήσασά ποι καὶ συναθροι-
σθεῖσα περὶ ἕν τι τοῦ σώματος μόριον ἀνθί-
σταται τῷ κτείνοντι καὶ πηδᾷ καὶ ἀγανακτεῖ,
μέχρις ἂν ὥσπερ πῦρ ἐγκατασβεσθῇ παντάπασι καὶ ἀπόληται.

Δέησις δ᾽ οὐκ ἔστιν οὐδ᾽ οἴκτου παραίτη-
σις οὐδ᾽ ἐξομολόγησις ἥττης, οὐδὲ δουλεύει
λέων λέοντι καὶ ἵππος ἵππῳ δι᾽ ἀνανδρίαν,
ὥσπερ ἄνθρωπος ἀνθρώπῳ, τὴν τῆς δειλίας
ἐπώνυμον εὐκόλως ἐνασπαζόμενος. ὅσα δ᾽
ἄνθρωποι πάγαις ἢ δόλοις ἐχειρώσαντο, τὰ
μὲν ἤδη τέλεια τροφὴν ἀπωσάμενα καὶ πρὸς

with it. Yet you will notice that the contests of animals one against another and against you humans are without guile and artifice. They fight their battles openly with naked courage from true valor. They're not compelled to fight by law, nor do they fight from fear of indictment for desertion, but naturally resist being conquered. Animals remain steadfast to the very end and retain an unyielding spirit. They are not vanquished, nor do they relinquish their lives, even when physically overpowered and dying in battle. Often, when animals are dying, their strength retreats inward to its seat of courage, gathering itself into some one part of its body to oppose whoever is killing it and leaps forth with vehemence until, like a fire, it is extinguished and dies down completely.[16]

Animals don't beg or plead for mercy. Nor do they admit defeat. Lion never serves as slave to lion, nor horse to horse through cowardice,[17] as does one human to another, readily accepting the eponym for timidity.[18] Among animals that humans subdue with snares and by stealth ones that

δίψαν ἐγκαρτερήσαντα τὸν πρὸ δουλείας
ἐπάγεται καὶ ἀγαπᾷ θάνατον· νεοσσοῖς δὲ καὶ
σκύμνοις τούτων, δι' ἡλικίαν εὐαγώγοις καὶ
ἁπαλοῖς οὖσιν, πολλὰ καὶ ἀπατηλὰ μειλίγ-
ματα καὶ ὑποπεττεύματα προφέροντες καὶ
καταφαρμάττοντες, ἡδονῶν παρὰ φύσιν γευ-
όμενα καὶ διαίτης ἀδρανῆ χρόνῳ κατειργά-
σαντο, ἕως προσεδέξαντο καὶ ὑπέμειναν
τὴν καλουμένην ἐξημέρωσιν ὥσπερ ἀπογυ-
ναίκωσιν τοῦ θυμοειδοῦς. Οἷς δὴ μάλιστα
δῆλον ὅτι τὰ θηρία πρὸς τὸ θαρρεῖν εὖ πέ-
φυκε. τοῖς δ' ἀνθρώποις ἡ παρρησία καὶ παρὰ
φύσιν ἐστίν·

ἐκεῖθεν δ' ἄν, ὦ βέλτιστ' Ὀδυσσεῦ, μάλιστα καταμάθοις· ἐν γὰρ τοῖς θηρίοις ἰσορ-
ροπεῖ πρὸς ἀλκὴν ἡ φύσις καὶ τὸ θῆλυ τοῦ
ἄρρενος οὐδὲν ἀποδεῖ πονεῖν τε τοὺς ἐπὶ
τοῖς ἀναγκαίοις πόνους ἀγωνίζεσθαί τε τοὺς
ὑπὲρ τῶν τέκνων ἀγῶνας. ἀλλά που Κρομ-
μυωνίαν τινὰ σῦν ἀκούεις, ἢ πράγματα
πολλά, θῆλυ θηρίον οὖσα, τῷ Θησεῖ παρέ-
σχε· καὶ τὴν Σφίγγα ἐκείνην οὐκ ἂν ὤνησεν
ἡ σοφία περὶ τὸ Φίκιον ἄνω καθεζομένην,
αἰνίγματα καὶ γρίφους πλέκουσαν, εἰ μὴ ῥώμῃ

are fully grown refuse food and endure thirst
to bring on death, which they welcome, in
place of slavery. Whereas to animals' chicks
and cubs, because they are docile and gentle on account of their age, humans offer
deceptions, tasty morsels, and inducements
to enchant them. Once they get a taste of
these unnatural pleasures and this mode of
life, in time they are rendered weak until
they accept and tolerate their so-called
taming, which amounts to an emasculation
of their spirited part. These facts prove that,
by nature, animals are courageous. Whereas,
among humans, boldness[19] is contrary to
nature.

Based on that, excellent Odysseus, you
should take special note of this, that, among
animals, nature is equal with respect to
strength and that the female is in no way inferior to the male, but also endures hard-
ships in the struggle for survival and fights
contests on behalf of her offspring. I sup-
pose you've heard of the sow from Crommyon, a female animal that caused Theseus
so much trouble?[20] Similarly, wisdom would
have done the famous Sphinx no good, seated

καὶ ἀνδρείᾳ πολὺ τῶν Καδμείων ἐπεκράτει. ἐκεῖ δέ που καὶ Τευμησίαν[8] ἀλώπεκα "μέρμερον χρῆμα" καὶ πλησίον ὄφιν τῷ Ἀπόλλωνι περὶ τοῦ χρηστηρίου μονομαχοῦσαν ἐν Δελφοῖς γενέσθαι λέγουσι.

τὴν δ' Αἴθην ὁ βασιλεὺς ὑμῶν ἔλαβε παρὰ τοῦ Σικυωνίου μισθὸν ἀστρατείας, ἄριστα βουλευσάμενος ὃς δειλοῦ προυτίμησεν ἀνδρὸς ἵππον ἀγαθὴν καὶ φιλόνικον. αὐτὸς δὲ καὶ παρδάλεις καὶ λεαίνας πολλάκις ἑώρακας, ὡς οὐδέν τι τὰ θήλεα τοῖς ἄρρεσιν ὑφίεται θυμοῦ καὶ ἀλκῆς· ὥσπερ ἡ σὴ γυνή, σοῦ πολεμοῦντος, οἴκοι κάθηται πρὸς ἐσχάρᾳ πυρός, οὐκ ἂν οὐδ' ὅσον αἱ χελιδόνες ἀμυνομένη τοὺς ἐπ' αὐτὴν καὶ τὸν οἶκον βαδίζοντας, καὶ ταῦτα Λάκαινα οὖσα. τί οὖν ἔτι σοι λέγω τὰς Καρίνας ἢ Μαιονίδας; ἀλλ' ἐκ τούτων γε δῆλόν ἐστιν, ὅτι τοῖς ἀνδράσιν οὐ φύσει μέτεστι τῆς ἀνδρείας· μετῆν γὰρ ἂν ὁμοίως καὶ ταῖς γυναιξὶν ἀλκῆς.

high on Mount Phicium plaiting her riddles and ciphers, if she did not hold tremendous sway over the sons of Cadmus through bravery and strength.[21] Somewhere in that region, too, they say arose the vixen of Teumessus, "a mischievous monster,"[22] and, hard by, the snake who fought in single combat with Apollo for control over the oracle at Delphi.[23]

Your king Agamemnon accepted the horse Aethe from the man from Sicyon[24] as payment for military deferment. He made a good choice in preferring a fine and feisty mare to a cowardly man! You yourself have seen panthers and lionesses, how the females in no way yield to the males in spirit and strength. Your wife, by contrast, sits at home by the hearth while you are off at war and with not so much vigor as a barn swallow does she ward off the men who are going after her and your household—this despite being a Spartan.[25] Why bother mentioning Maeonian and Carian women?[26] From these examples alone it is clear that men do not possess innate courage and even if they did, women would lay an equal claim to strength.

ὥσθ᾽ ὑμεῖς, κατὰ νόμων ἀνάγκην οὐχ ἑκού-
σιον οὐδὲ βουλομένην ἀλλὰ δουλεύουσαν
ἔθεσι καὶ ψόγοις καὶ δόξαις ἐπήλυσι καὶ λόγοις πλαττομένην, μελετᾶτε ἀνδρείαν· καὶ
τοὺς πόνους ὑφίστασθε καὶ τοὺς κινδύνους,
οὐ πρὸς ταῦτα θαρροῦντες ἀλλὰ τῷ ἕτερα
μᾶλλον τούτων δεδιέναι. ὥσπερ οὖν τῶν σῶν
ἑταίρων ὁ φθάσας πρῶτος ἐπὶ τὴν ἐλαφρὰν
ἀνίσταται κώπην, οὐ καταφρονῶν ἐκείνης
ἀλλὰ δεδιὼς καὶ φεύγων τὴν βαρυτέραν·
οὕτως ὁ πληγὴν ὑπομένων, ἵνα μὴ λάβῃ
τραύματα, καὶ πρὸ αἰκίας τινὸς ἢ θανάτου πο-
λέμιόν τιν᾽ ἀμυνόμενος οὐ πρὸς ταῦτα θαρ-
ραλέος ἀλλὰ πρὸς ἐκεῖνα δειλός ἐστιν. οὕτω
δ᾽ ἀναφαίνεται ὑμῖν ἡ μὲν ἀνδρεία δειλία
φρόνιμος οὖσα, τὸ δὲ θάρσος φόβος ἐπι-
στήμην ἔχων τοῦ δι᾽ ἑτέρων ἕτερα φεύγειν.

ὅλως δέ, εἰ πρὸς ἀνδρείαν οἴεσθε βελτίους
εἶναι τῶν θηρίων, τί ποθ᾽ ὑμῶν οἱ ποιηταὶ τοὺς
κράτιστα τοῖς πολεμίοις μαχομένους "λυκό-
φρονας" καὶ "θυμολέοντας" καὶ "συῒ εἰκέλους

It follows, then, that you humans exercise a kind of courage that is compelled by law.[27] It is not voluntary or freely chosen but subservient to custom, fear of censure, and molded by others' opinions and rationales. You submit to dangers and toils not out of confidence in the face of such things but for fear of some worse alternative. It's like that man among your companions who is the first to take his place at the oar—a light oar—not because he is indifferent to its size, but because he is afraid of the heavier oar and so avoids that one. So, too, the person who submits to a blow in order not to be wounded, or who fends off a foe to avoid torture or death: he is not being courageous in the face of such things; he's being cowardly vis-à-vis the alternative. Thus, it turns out your courage is in fact calculated cowardice and your fierceness merely fear that is conversant with ways to escape one set of consequences via another.

In short, if you humans think you are better than animals in courage, why do your poets call the best combatants "wolf-minded" and "lionhearted" and "like a boar

ἀλκὴν" προσαγορεύουσιν, ἀλλ᾽ οὐ λέοντά
τις αὐτῶν "ἀνθρωπόθυμον," οὐ σῦν "ἀνδρὶ
εἴκελον ἀλκὴν" προσαγορεύει· ἀλλ᾽ ὥσπερ
οἶμαι τοὺς ταχεῖς "ποδηνέμους" καὶ τοὺς
καλοὺς "θεοειδεῖς" ὑπερβαλλόμενοι ταῖς
εἰκόσιν ὀνομάζουσιν, οὕτω τῶν δεινῶν μά-
χεσθαι πρὸς τὰ κρείττονα ποιοῦνται τὰς
ἀφομοιώσεις.

αἴτιον δέ, ὅτι τῆς μὲν ἀνδρείας οἷον βαφή
τις ὁ θυμός ἐστι καὶ στόμωμα· τούτῳ δ᾽ ἀκράτῳ
τὰ θηρία χρῆται πρὸς τοὺς ἀγῶνας, ὑμῖν δὲ
προσμιγνύμενος πρὸς τὸν λογισμὸν ὥσπερ
οἶνος πρὸς ὕδωρ ἐξίσταται παρὰ τὰ δεινὰ καὶ
ἀπολείπει τὸν καιρόν. ἔνιοι δ᾽ ὑμῶν οὐδ᾽ ὅλως
φασὶ χρῆναι παραλαμβάνειν ἐν ταῖς μάχαις
τὸν θυμὸν ἀλλ᾽ ἐκποδὼν θεμένους νήφοντι
χρῆσθαι τῷ λογισμῷ, πρὸς μὲν σωτηρίας
ἀσφάλειαν ὀρθῶς, πρὸς δ᾽ ἀλκὴν καὶ ἄμυναν
αἴσχιστα λέγοντες. πῶς γὰρ οὐκ ἄτοπον αἰτιᾶ-
σθαι μὲν ὑμᾶς τὴν φύσιν, ὅτι μὴ κέντρα προσέ-
φυσε τοῖς σώμασι μηδ᾽ ἀμυντηρίους ὀδόντας
μηδ᾽ ἀγκύλους ὄνυχας, αὐτοὺς δὲ τῆς ψυχῆς
τὸ σύμφυτον ἀφαιρεῖν ὅπλον καὶ κολούειν;

in strength"?[28] None of them ever addresses a lion as "human-hearted" or a pig as "like a man in strength." I think that just as poets exaggerate by labeling swift people "wind-footed" and beautiful people "godlike," so too they make comparisons of fearsome fighters with creatures that are stronger than the comparands.

And the reason is that the spirit is like the tempered cutting edge of courage.[29] Animals' spirits are undiluted, whereas, for you humans, calculation has been mixed in, as wine with water,[30] so your spirit shirks when faced with danger and fails you at the critical moment. Some of you even say one shouldn't employ one's spirit in battles entirely but should keep it out of one's way and use sober calculation. When it comes to self-preservation, that's correct. But if it's a question of valor and defense, what they argue is most ill suited. How is it not absurd for you humans to blame Nature for not causing stingers to grow on your bodies, nor defensive fangs, nor curved talons, and yet remove and hold in check your soul's innate weaponry?[31]

5. ΟΔ.

Παπαί, ὦ Γρύλλε, δεινός μοι δοκεῖς γεγονέναι σοφιστής, ὅς γε καὶ νῦν ἐκ τῆς συηνίας φθεγγόμενος οὕτω νεανικῶς πρὸς τὴν ὑπόθεσιν ἐπικεχείρηκας. ἀλλὰ τί οὐ περὶ τῆς σωφροσύνης ἐφεξῆς διεξῆλθες;

ΓΡ.

Ὅτι ᾤμην σε τῶν εἰρημένων πρότερον ἐπιλήψεσθαι· σὺ δὲ σπεύδεις ἀκοῦσαι τὸ περὶ τῆς σωφροσύνης, ἐπεὶ σωφρονεστάτης μὲν ἀνὴρ εἶ γυναικός, ἀπόδειξιν δὲ σωφροσύνης αὐτὸς οἴει δεδωκέναι, τῶν Κίρκης ἀφροδισίων περιφρονήσας. κἂν τούτῳ μὲν οὐδενὸς τῶν θηρίων διαφέρεις πρὸς ἐγκράτειαν· οὐδὲ γὰρ ἐκεῖνα τοῖς κρείττοσιν ἐπιθυμεῖ πλησιάζειν ἀλλὰ καὶ τὰς ἡδονὰς καὶ τοὺς ἔρωτας πρὸς τὰ ὁμόφυλα ποιεῖται. οὐ θαυμαστὸν οὖν ἐστιν, εἰ καθάπερ ὁ Μενδήσιος ἐν Αἰγύπτῳ τράγος λέγεται πολλαῖς καὶ καλαῖς συνειργνύμενος γυναιξὶν οὐκ εἶναι μίγνυσθαι πρόθυμος ἀλλὰ πρὸς τὰς αἶγας ἐπτοῆσθαι μᾶλλον, οὕτω σὺ χαίρων ἀφροδισίοις συνήθεσιν οὐ θέλεις ἄνθρωπος ὢν θεᾷ συγκαθεύδειν. τὴν δὲ Πηνελόπης σωφροσύνην μυρίαι κορῶναι

ODYSSEUS

My, my, Gryllus, you strike me as having once been a fearsome rhetorician! Despite speaking in your current, piggish state, you attack your theme with such vigor! But why did you not continue with the next virtue in line, self-control?

GRYLLUS

Because I thought you would first counter-attack what I have said. You are anxious to hear about self-control, I surmise, because you are the husband of a wife with as much self-control as there is out there, and you think that you yourself have exhibited proof of your own self-control by despising a sexual relationship with Circe.[32] But in this you are no different from any animal in terms of self-mastery. For they don't desire to have intercourse with their superiors either but take pleasure and make love with their own species. So it's no surprise that, just like the billy goat of Mendes in Egypt, who, when penned in with many beautiful women is said not to be eager to mate with them, but gets more excited by the nanny

κρώζουσαι γέλωτα θήσονται καὶ καταφρο-
νήσουσιν, ὧν ἑκάστη,[3] ἂν ἀποθάνῃ ὁ ἄρρην,
οὐκ ὀλίγον χρόνον ἀλλ᾽ ἐννέα χηρεύει γενεὰς
ἀνθρώπων· ὥστε σοι τὴν καλὴν Πηνελόπην
ἐννάκις ἀπολείπεσθαι τῷ σωφρονεῖν ἧς βούλει
κορώνης.

6. Ἀλλ᾽ ἐπεί σε μὴ λέληθα σοφιστὴς ὤν,
φέρε χρήσωμαι τάξει τινὶ τοῦ λόγου, τῆς μὲν
σωφροσύνης ὅρον θέμενος, κατὰ γένος δὲ
τὰς ἐπιθυμίας διελόμενος. ἡ μὲν οὖν σωφρο-
σύνη βραχύτης τίς ἐστιν ἐπιθυμιῶν καὶ τάξις,
ἀναιροῦσα μὲν τὰς ἐπεισάκτους καὶ περιτ-
τάς, καιρῷ δὲ καὶ μετριότητι κοσμοῦσα τὰς
ἀναγκαίας. ταῖς δ᾽ ἐπιθυμίαις ἐνορᾷς που
μυρίαν διαφοράν . . . καὶ τὴν περὶ τὴν βρῶσιν
καὶ τὴν πόσιν ἅμα τῷ φυσικῷ καὶ τὸ ἀνα-
γκαῖον ἔχουσαν· αἱ δὲ τῶν ἀφροδισίων αἷς
ἀρχὰς ἡ φύσις ἐνδίδωσιν, ἔστι δέ που καὶ μὴ
χρώμενον ἔχειν ἱκανῶς ἀπαλλαγέντα, φυσι-
καὶ μὲν οὐκ ἀναγκαῖαι δ᾽ ἐκλήθησαν. τὸ δὲ
τῶν μήτ᾽ ἀναγκαίων μήτε φυσικῶν ἀλλ᾽

goats,[33] so too you, a human man, enjoy sex with what is familiar and are loath to sleep with a goddess. As for Penelope's self-control, ten thousand cawing crows will make a laughingstock of it and hold it in contempt since each of *them*, if their male mate dies, remains a widow, not for a short time, but for nine human generations.[34] Thus, in terms of self-control, your fair Penelope falls nine times short of any crow you please!

Now, then, since you've gathered that I'm a rhetorician, let me proceed with the argument in an orderly fashion by defining self-control and analyzing desires according to their kind. Self-control is a kind of narrowing and organizing of desires that eliminates those that are alien and superfluous and sets in order those that are essential by observing proper measure and by knowing when to apply them. You'll see a host of differences among desires. . . . [35] The desire to eat and drink, for example, is both natural and necessary. The desire for sex, on the other hand, though it is perfectly natural in origin, were it to be deprived, one

ἔξωθεν ὑπὸ δόξης κενῆς δι' ἀπειροκαλίαν
ἐπικεχυμένων γένος ὑμῶν μὲν ὀλίγου δεῖν
τὰς φυσικὰς ἀπέκρυψεν ὑπὸ πλήθους ἁπά-
σας, ἔχει δὲ καθάπερ ξένος ὄχλος ἔπηλυς ἐν
δήμῳ καταβιαζόμενος πρὸς τοὺς ἐγγενεῖς
πολίτας. τὰ δὲ θηρία παντάπασιν ἀβάτους καὶ
ἀνεπιμίκτους ἔχοντα τοῖς ἐπεισάκτοις πάθεσι
τὰς ψυχὰς καὶ τοῖς βίοις πόρρω τῆς κενῆς
δόξης ὥσπερ θαλάσσης ἀπῳκισμένα· τῷ μὲν
γλαφυρῶς καὶ περιττῶς διάγειν ἀπολείπεται,
τὸ δὲ σωφρονεῖν καὶ μᾶλλον εὐνομεῖσθαι ταῖς
ἐπιθυμίαις, οὔτε πολλαῖς συνοικούσαις οὔτ'
ἀλλοτρίαις, σφόδρα διαφυλάττεται.

Ἐμὲ γοῦν ποτε καὶ αὐτὸν οὐχ ἧττον ἢ σὲ
νῦν ἐξέπληττε μὲν χρυσὸς ὡς κτῆμα τῶν
ἄλλων οὐδενὶ παραβλητόν, ἥρει δ' ἄργυρος
καὶ ἐλέφας· ὁ δὲ πλεῖστα τούτων κεκτημένος
ἐδόκει μακάριός τις εἶναι καὶ θεοφιλὴς ἀνήρ,
εἴτε Φρὺξ ἦν εἴτε Κὰρ τοῦ Δόλωνος ἀγεννέ-
στερος καὶ τοῦ Πριάμου βαρυποτμότερος.

could get on perfectly well without, and so it would be classified as natural, but not essential. But that species of desires that are neither essential nor natural but pour in from outside to satisfy your empty fancies[36] and vulgar tastes has, by sheer number, hidden from sight almost all natural desires—a situation not unlike a mob of foreigners from abroad overpowering native citizens.[37] Animals, however, possess souls that are entirely inaccessible and unvisited by outside influences and live settled lives as far from empty fancies as one would who lived far from the sea.[38] Animals may fall short when it comes to dainty, excessive lifestyles, but they stoutly guard their self-control and the regulation of their desires, and those desires that do reside in them are neither many nor foreign.

There was once a time when I myself, no less than you now, was transfixed with gold as if it were an unparalleled possession. Silver and ivory captivated me, too. A man who acquired the most of such things seemed to me fortunate and one of the gods' favorites. It didn't matter if he was a Phrygian

ἐνταῦθα δ᾽ ἀνηρτημένος ἀεὶ ταῖς ἐπιθυμίας οὔτε χάριν οὔθ᾽ ἡδονὴν ἀπὸ τῶν ἄλλων πραγμάτων ἀφθόνων ὄντων καὶ ἱκανῶν ἐκαρπούμην, μεμφόμενος τὸν ἐμαυτοῦ βίον, ὡς τῶν μεγίστων ἐνδεὴς καὶ ἄμοιρος ἀγαθῶν ἀπολελειμμένος.

τοιγαροῦν σ᾽ ὡς μέμνημαι ἐν Κρήτῃ θεασάμενος ἀμπεχόνῃ κεκοσμημένον πανηγυρικῶς, οὐ τὴν φρόνησιν ἐζήλουν οὐδὲ τὴν ἀρετήν, ἀλλὰ τοῦ χιτῶνος εἰργασμένου περιττῶς τὴν λεπτότητα καὶ τῆς χλαμύδος οὔσης ἁλουργοῦ τὴν οὐλότητα καὶ τὸ κάλλος ἀγαπῶν καὶ τεθηπώς (εἶχε δέ τι καὶ ἡ πόρπη χρυσὸς οὖσα παίγνιον οἶμαι τορείαις διηκριβωμένον) καὶ εἱπόμην γεγοητευμένος, ὥσπερ αἱ γυναῖκες. ἀλλὰ νῦν ἀπηλλαγμένος ἐκείνων τῶν κενῶν δοξῶν καὶ κεκαθαρμένος χρυσὸν μὲν καὶ ἄργυρον ὥσπερ τοὺς ἄλλους λίθους περιορῶν ὑπερβαίων, ταῖς δὲ σαῖς χλανίσι καὶ τάπησιν οὐδὲν ἂν μὰ Δί᾽ ἥδιον ἢ βαθεῖ καὶ μαλθακῷ πηλῷ μεστὸς

or a Carian, more ignoble than a Dolon, or more ill-fated than a Priam.[39] Consequently, I reaped no joy or pleasure from the other good things in my life, which were sufficient, even plentiful, but was continually in suspense, hung up by my desires. I found fault with my life, thinking myself in need of the greatest things, even unluckily deprived of good things.

That's why, I remember well, when I saw you once on Crete adorned in fancy garb, as if for a festival, I was not jealous of your good sense or virtue. It was the soft hand of your sumptuously woven cloak and the beautiful wool of your purple mantle that I gawked and gaped at. (It had a golden clasp, too, I believe, with a whimsical design intricately carved in relief.) I followed you about, entranced, like a woman. But now, delivered and purified of those empty fancies, I walk right past silver and gold, regarding them as any other hunks of stone. And as for your cloaks and duvets, there's nothing sweeter, I swear, when I'm full, than to bed down to sleep in deep, soft mud. Not

ὧν ἐγκατακλιθείην ἀναπαυόμενος. τῶν δὲ
τοιούτων τῶν ἐπεισάκτων ἐπιθυμιῶν οὐδεμία
ταῖς ἡμετέραις ἐνοικίζεται ψυχαῖς· ἀλλὰ τὰ
μὲν πλεῖστα ταῖς ἀναγκαίαις ὁ βίος ἡμῶν
ἐπιθυμίαις καὶ ἡδοναῖς διοικεῖται, ταῖς δ᾽ οὐκ
ἀναγκαίαις ἀλλὰ φυσικαῖς μόνον οὔτ᾽ ἀτά-
κτως οὔτ᾽ ἀπλήστως ὁμιλοῦμεν.
7. Καὶ ταύτας γε πρῶτον διέλθωμεν. ἡ μὲν
οὖν πρὸς τὰ εὐώδη καὶ κινοῦντα ταῖς ἀποφο-
ραῖς τὴν ὄσφρησιν οἰκείως ἡδονὴ πρὸς τῷ τὸ
ὄφελος καὶ προῖκα καὶ ἁπλοῦν ἔχειν ἅμα
χρείαν τινὰ συμβάλλεται τῇ διαγνώσει τῆς
τροφῆς. ἡ μὲν γὰρ γλῶττα τοῦ γλυκέος καὶ
δριμέος καὶ αὐστηροῦ γνώμων ἐστί τε καὶ
λέγεται, ὅταν τῷ γευστικῷ προσμιγέντες οἱ
χυμοὶ σύγχυσίν τινα λάβωσιν· ἡ δ᾽ ὄσφρησις
ἡμῶν πρὸ τῶν χυμῶν γνώμων οὖσα τῆς δυ-
νάμεως ἑκάστου πολὺ τῶν βασιλικῶν προ-
γευστῶν σκεπτικώτερον διαισθανομένη, τὸ
μὲν οἰκεῖον εἴσω παρίησι τὸ δ᾽ ἀλλότριον
ἀπελαύνει καὶ οὐκ ἐᾷ θιγεῖν οὐδὲ λυπῆσαι
τὴν γεῦσιν ἀλλὰ διαβάλλει καὶ κατηγορεῖ τὴν
φαυλότητα πρὶν ἢ βλαβῆναι· τἆλλα δ᾽ οὐκ
ἐνοχλεῖ, καθάπερ ὑμῖν, τὰ θυμιάματα καὶ κιν-
νάμωμα καὶ νάρδους καὶ φύλλα καὶ καλάμους
Ἀραβικούς, μετὰ δεινῆς τινος δευσοποιοῦ

one of those alien desires makes its home in *our* souls. The housekeeping of our lives is managed for the most part by pleasures and desires that are natural and essential. As for those pleasures that are inessential, but natural, we do not engage in them without discipline, nor to excess.

Let us survey these pleasures. Take first the pleasure derived from scents. When fragrances are emitted, they naturally activate our sense of smell. In addition to being a free and simple benefit, smell likewise serves a purpose in distinguishing foods. Whereas the tongue is said to be (and is) an indicator of what is sweet, or bitter, or tart, whenever flavors mix and meld, as it were, with the taste buds, our sense of smell is an indicator, even before flavor, of the quality of each food item that is far more perceptive than the most discriminating royal taster. It lets enter what is native to us but expels what is foreign and does not allow it to touch or trouble the sense of taste. It accuses and denounces poor quality before it does any harm. Overall, we do not trouble ourselves about smells as you do.

καὶ φαρμακίδος τέχνης, ἢ μυρεψικῆς ὄνομα,
συνάγειν εἰς ταὐτὸ καὶ συμφυρᾶν ἀναγκά-
ζουσα, χρημάτων πολλῶν ἡδυπάθειαν ἄναν-
δρον καὶ κορασιώδη καὶ πρὸς οὐδὲν οὐδαμῶς
χρήσιμον ὠνουμένοις.

ἀλλὰ καίπερ οὖσα τοιαύτη διέφθαρκεν
οὐ μόνον πάσας γυναῖκας ἀλλὰ καὶ τῶν ἀν-
δρῶν ἤδη τοὺς πλείστους, ὡς μηδὲ ταῖς
αὐτῶν ἐθέλειν συγγίνεσθαι γυναιξίν, εἰ μὴ
μύρων ὑμῖν ὀδωδυῖαι καὶ διαπασμάτων εἰς
ταὐτὸ φοιτῶεν. ἀλλὰ κάπρους τε σύες καὶ
τράγους αἶγες καὶ τἆλλα θήλεα τοὺς συν-
νόμους αὐτῶν ταῖς ἰδίαις ὀσμαῖς ἐπάγεται,
δρόσου τε καθαρᾶς καὶ λειμώνων ὀδωδότα
καὶ χλόης συμφέρεται πρὸς τοὺς γάμους ὑπὸ
κοινῆς φιλοφροσύνης, οὐχὶ θρυπτόμεναι
μὲν αἱ θήλειαι καὶ προϊσχόμεναι τῆς ἐπιθυμίας ἀπάτας καὶ γοητείας καὶ ἀρνήσεις, οἱ δ᾽
ἄρρενες ὑπ᾽ οἴστρου καὶ μαργότητος ὠνού-
μενοι μισθῶν καὶ πόνου καὶ λατρείας τὸ τῆς
γενέσεως ἔργον, ἄδολον δὲ σὺν καιρῷ καὶ
ἄμισθον Ἀφροδίτην μετιόντες, ἢ καθ᾽ ὥραν

You feel compelled to gather and blend into the same concoction incense—cinnamon, spikenard, herbs, and aromatic reeds from Arabia—and combine that with the skilled craft of a dyer or sorceress to produce what is called ointment making. This you purchase at great expense—an effeminate luxury, unworthy of a man, and of no use whatsoever.

And, although that is its essence, it nonetheless corrupts not only every woman but lately most of you men as well, to the point where you're unwilling to sleep with your own wives unless they come to bed reeking of myrrh and scented powders, whereas sows attract boars; and nanny goats, bucks; and other female animals their partners by their own unique scents—perfumes distilled of pure dew and grassy meadows—and are brought together in matrimony by mutual affection. Our females are not coy and do not hold forth with deceptions, sweet talk, or refusals. Our males aren't driven mad with lust. Animals don't purchase the work of procreation with payments, labor, or servitude. Rather, both parties come together

ἔτους ὥσπερ φυτῶν βλάστην ἐγείρουσα τῶν ζῴων τὴν ἐπιθυμίαν εὐθὺς ἔσβεσεν, οὔτε τοῦ θήλεος προσιεμένου μετὰ τὴν κύησιν οὔτε πειρῶντος ἔτι τοῦ ἄρρενος. οὕτω μικρὰν ἔχει καὶ ἀσθενῆ τιμὴν ἡδονὴ παρ' ἡμῖν, τὸ δ' ὅλον ἡ φύσις. . . .

9. . . . ἡ τῶν θηρίων φρόνησις τῶν μὲν ἀχρήστων καὶ ματαίων τεχνῶν οὐδεμιᾷ χώραν δίδωσι, τὰς δ' ἀναγκαίας οὐκ ἐπεισάκτους παρ' ἑτέρων οὐδὲ μισθοῦ διδακτὰς οὐδὲ κολ-λῶσα μελέτη καὶ συμπηγνύουσα γλίσχρως τῶν θεωρημάτων ἕκαστον πρὸς ἕκαστον ἀλλ' αὐτόθεν ἐξ αὑτῆς οἷον ἰθαγενεῖς καὶ συμ-φύτους ἀναδίδωσι. τοὺς μὲν γὰρ Αἰγυπτίους πάντας ἰατροὺς ἀκούομεν εἶναι, τῶν δὲ ζῴων ἕκαστον οὐ μόνον πρὸς ἴσαιν αὐτότεχνόν ἐστιν ἀλλὰ καὶ πρὸς διατροφὴν καὶ πρὸς ἀλκὴν θήραν τε καὶ φυλακὴν καὶ μουσικῆς ὅσον ἑκάστῳ προσήκει κατὰ φύσιν. παρὰ τίνος γὰρ ἡμεῖς ἐμάθομεν νοσοῦντες ἐπὶ τοὺς ποταμοὺς χάριν τῶν καρκίνων βαδίζειν; τίς δὲ τὰς χελώνας ἐδίδαξε τῆς ἔχεως φαγούσας τὴν ὀρίγανον ἐπεσθίειν; τίς δὲ τὰς Κρητικὰς

in a sexual union that is without guile and free of charge, which awakens our desire in the season of spring, like the blossoming of plants, whereafter it is immediately quenched. The female does not receive her mate after she has conceived; nor does the male attempt to mount her. That's how weak and small we think pleasure is. Nature, rather, is our whole concern. . . .

Animal intelligence affords no place to useless, pointless arts. Essential skills are not imported from others, from outside, nor are we taught them for a price. We are not clingy in that we do not glue or nail down an individual to the practice of just one field of inquiry. *Our* intelligence produces skills of its own accord, spontaneously, as if those skills were innate and authentic. We hear that everyone in Egypt is a physician.[40] Well, each of us animals is self-taught, not only in medicine, but also in foddering, in hunting, in providing protection, and in music (to the extent that any of us is so inclined by nature).[41] From whom did we pigs learn to waddle down to the river when sick in search of crabs? Who taught turtles to eat oregano

αἶγας, ὅταν περιπέσωσι τοῖς τοξεύμασι, τὸ δί-
κταμνον διώκειν, οὗ βρωθέντος ἐκβάλλουσι
τὰς ἀκίδας; ἂν γὰρ εἴπῃς, ὅπερ ἀληθές ἐστι,
τούτων διδάσκαλον εἶναι τὴν φύσιν, εἰς τὴν
κυριωτάτην καὶ σοφωτάτην ἀρχὴν ἀναφέρεις
τὴν τῶν θηρίων φρόνησιν· ἣν εἰ μὴ λόγον οἴεσθε δεῖν μηδὲ φρόνησιν καλεῖν, ὥρα σκοπεῖν
ὄνομα κάλλιον αὐτῇ καὶ τιμιώτερον, ὥσπερ
ἀμέλει καὶ δι᾽ ἔργων ἀμείνονα καὶ θαυμασιω-
τέραν παρέχεται τὴν δύναμιν· … καταδὺς δ᾽
εἰς τουτὶ τὸ σῶμα θαυμάζω τοὺς λόγους ἐκεί-
νους οἷς ἀνεπειθόμην ὑπὸ τῶν σοφιστῶν
ἄλογα καὶ ἀνόητα πάντα πλὴν ἀνθρώπου
νομίζειν …

after eating a viper? And who taught the goats of Crete, when they are pierced by arrows, to go in search of dittany, which makes the arrowheads pop out once they've eaten some?[42] If you speak the truth and say that Nature is their teacher, then you are tracing the intelligence of animals back to the most authoritative and wisest origin. And if you humans don't think it ought to be called reason or intelligence, see to it that you find a finer and more honorable name for it, since what we have certainly displays a power through its works that is even better and more amazing. . . . Indeed, ever since entering this body you see here, I am shocked at those arguments by which I had been persuaded by the rhetoricians to think that all animals except the human being are irrational and mindless. . . .

12. Abstinence Makes the Heart Grow Fonder (Porphyry, *On Abstaining from Animals* Book 3, Abridged)

Ostensibly a philosophical case for vegetarianism, this remarkable excerpt from a longer, somewhat repetitive treatise by Porphyry of Tyre (ca. 234–305 CE) espouses more broadly a Greek version of the Jainist doctrine of ahimsa *("do no harm"). Porphyry cribs various sources here (Aristotle and Plutarch loom large) to argue that animals possess rationality and thus rights. Perhaps his most powerful observation is that the just treatment of animals makes us better human beings.*

*Porphyry's work, as transmitted in the eighteenth-century treatise by the Neoplatonist Thomas Taylor (*A Vindication of the Rights of Brutes, *1792), is mentioned by Peter Singer in the opening pages of his classic* Animal Liberation *(1975). Singer, a bellwether of the modern animal rights movement, saw Taylor's work as a parody of Mary Wollstonecraft's* A Vindication of the Rights of Women

1. Ὡς μὲν οὔτε πρὸς σωφροσύνην καὶ λιτότητα
οὔτε πρὸς εὐσέβειαν, αἳ μάλιστα πρὸς τὸν θεωρη-
τικὸν συντελοῦσι βίον, ἡ τῶν ἐμψύχων βρῶσις
συμβάλλεται, ἀλλὰ μᾶλλον ἐναντιοῦται, διὰ τῶν
φθασάντων, ὦ Φίρμε Καστρίκιε, δυεῖν βιβλίων
ἀπεδείξαμεν. τῆς δὲ δικαιοσύνης τὸ κάλλιστον ἐν
τῇ πρὸς τοὺς θεοὺς εὐσεβείᾳ κεκτημένης, ταύτης
δὲ ὡς ἔνι μάλιστα διὰ τῆς ἀποχῆς συνισταμένης,
οὐ δέος ἐστὶ περὶ τοῦ πρὸς ἀνθρώπους δικαίου, μή
πῃ τοῦτο παραθραύσωμεν, τήν γε πρὸς τοὺς θεοὺς
ὁσίαν διασῴζοντες. Σωκράτης μὲν οὖν πρὸς τοὺς
ἡδονὴν διαμφισβητοῦντας εἶναι τὸ τέλος, οὐδ' ἂν
πάντες, ἔφη, σύες καὶ τράγοι τούτῳ συναινῶσι,
πεισθήσεσθαι ἐν τῷ ἥδεσθαι τὸ εὐδαιμονῆμῶν
κεῖσθαι, ἔστ' ἂν νοῦς ἐν τοῖς πᾶσι κρατῇ· ἡμεῖς δέ,
οὐδ' ἂν πάντες λύκοι ἢ γῦπες τὴν κρεοφαγίαν δο-
κιμάζωσιν, οὐ συγχωρήσομεν τούτοις δίκαια λέγειν, ἔστ' ἂν ὁ ἄνθρωπος ἀβλαβὲς ᾖ φύσει καὶ
ἀφεκτικὸν τοῦ διὰ τῆς ἄλλων βλάβης αὑτῷ τὰς
ἡδονὰς πορίζεσθαι. ἐς οὖν τὸν περὶ τῆς δικαιοσύνης

from the same year, which in part it was. But Taylor's
tractate also used Porphyry to defend vegetarian-
ism and the just treatment of animals with consid-
erable vigor. Here, without the filter of parody, we
give Porphyry the chance to speak for himself.

In the previous two books, Firmus Castricius,[1]
I pointed out that eating animate creatures does not
further the cause of moderation, simplicity, or
piety, which are what bring a contemplative life to
perfection. In fact, it impedes this goal. Since the
best aspect of justice consists in showing piety
toward the gods, which is itself most effectively se-
cured through abstinence,[2] there is no reason to
worry that we could somehow violate justice in our
interactions with humans by observing holiness
concerning the gods. To those who contend that
pleasure is our end-all, Socrates replied that, even if
all pigs and goats would agree with that proposi-
tion, he would not be persuaded that our happiness
lies in pleasure, so long as intellect holds sway in
the universe.[3] Likewise, we, even if all wolves and
vultures approve of meat eating, will not agree that
what they say is just if a human being is to be a
creature harmless by nature and one that abstains
from furnishing pleasure to itself by harming

λόγον μεταβαίνοντες, ἐπείπερ ταύτην πρὸς τὰ
ὅμοια δεῖν μόνα παρατείνειν εἰρήκασιν οἱ ἀντιλέ-
γοντες, καὶ διὰ τοῦτο τὰ ἄλογα διαγράφουσι τῶν
ζῴων, φέρε ἡμεῖς τὴν ἀληθῆ τε ὁμοῦ καὶ Πυθα-
γόρειον δόξαν παραστήσωμεν, πᾶσαν ψυχήν, ᾗ
μέτεστιν αἰσθήσεως καὶ μνήμης, λογικὴν ἐπιδει-
κνύντες· τούτου γὰρ ἀποδειχθέντος εἰκότως δὴ
καὶ κατὰ τούτους πρὸς πᾶν ζῷον τὸ δίκαιον παρα-
τενοῦμεν. ἐροῦμεν δὲ τὰ παρὰ τοῖς παλαιοῖς συντό-
μως ἐπιτέμνοντες.

2. διττοῦ δὴ λόγου κατὰ τοὺς ἀπὸ τῆς στοᾶς
ὄντος, τοῦ μὲν ἐνδιαθέτου, τοῦ δὲ προφορικοῦ, καὶ
πάλιν τοῦ μὲν κατωρθωμένου, τοῦ δὲ ἡμαρτημέ-
νου, ποτέρου ἀποστεροῦσι τὰ ζῷα διαρθρῶσαι
προσῆκον. ἆρά γε τοῦ ὀρθοῦ μόνου, οὐχ ἁπλῶς δὲ
τοῦ λόγου; ἢ παντελῶς παντὸς τοῦ τε ἔσω καὶ τοῦ
ἔξω προϊόντος; ἐοίκασι δὴ τὴν παντελῆ στέρησιν
αὐτῶν κατηγορεῖν, οὐ τὴν τοῦ κατωρθωμένου
μόνον. οὕτω γὰρ ἂν οὐκ ἄλογα, λογικὰ δὲ ἦν ἔτι τὰ
ζῷα, καθάπερ σχεδὸν πάντες κατ᾽ αὐτοὺς οἱ ἄνθρωποι. σοφὸς μὲν γὰρ ἢ εἷς ἢ καὶ δύο κατ᾽ αὐτοὺς
γεγόνασιν, ἐν οἷς μόνοις ὁ λόγος κατώρθωται, οἱ δὲ
ἄλλοι φαῦλοι πάντες· κἂν οἳ μὲν ὦσι προκόπτο-
ντες, οἳ δὲ χύσιν τῆς φαυλότητος ἔχοντες, εἰ καὶ
πάντες ὁμοίως λογικοί· ὑπὸ δὲ τῆς φιλαυτίας

others. Therefore, let us shift the argument about justice: Our opponents say it can be extended only to creatures like ourselves and therefore discount animals for their lack of reason. Let us, rather, counterpropose the true view, which is also the Pythagorean view, that every soul that possesses perception and memory is rational.[4] Once we have proved that, it will then be reasonable for us to extend justice—even our opponents' notion of it—to every animal. But first we will recount, briefly and succinctly, the views of the ancients.

The Stoics teach that there are two kinds of *logos*,[5] one called internal and one expressive, and, in addition, that there is a correct kind of *logos* and a faulty one. It behooves us, then, to determine which of these they say that animals lack. Is it just the correct kind and not *logos* altogether, or is it both/and, that is, the inner *logos* and the kind that projects to the outside? They seem to be asserting that they lack *logos* entirely, not just the correct kind. And yet, even on their own terms, animals would still possess *logos*, not lack it, on the grounds that, in the Stoic view, nearly all humans are in the same position, for they hold that there have been only one or two persons in whom *logos* of the correct kind has

παρηγμένοι ἄλογα φασὶν τὰ ζῷα ἐφεξῆς τὰ ἄλλα σύμπαντα … καίτοι εἰ χρὴ τἀληθὲς εἰπεῖν, οὐ μόνον ἁπλῶς ὁ λόγος ἐν πᾶσι τοῖς ζῴοις θεωρεῖται, ἐν πολλοῖς δὲ αὐτῶν καὶ ὑποβολὰς ἔχων πρὸς τὸ τέλειον.

3. ἐπεὶ τοίνυν διττὸς ἦν, ὃ μὲν ἐν τῇ προφορᾷ, ὃ δὲ ἐν τῇ διαθέσει, ἀρξώμεθα πρό- τερον ἀπὸ τοῦ προφορικοῦ καὶ τοῦ κατὰ τὴν φωνὴν τεταγμένου. εἰ δὴ προφορικός ἐστι λόγος φωνὴ διὰ γλώττης σημαντικὴ τῶν ἔνδον καὶ κατὰ ψυχὴν παθῶν· κοινοτάτη γὰρ ἡ ἀπόδοσις αὕτη καὶ αἱρέσεως οὐδέπω ἐχομένη, ἀλλὰ μόνον τῆς τοῦ λόγου ἐννοίας· τί τούτου ἄπεστι τῶν ζῴων ὅσα φθέγγεται; τί δὲ οὐχὶ καὶ ἃ πάσχει τι, πρότερον καὶ πρὶν εἰπεῖν ὃ μέλλει, διενοήθη; λέγω δὴ διάνοιαν τὸ ἐν τῇ ψυχῇ κατὰ σιγὴν φωνούμενον. τοῦ τοίνυν ὑπὸ τῆς γλώττης φωνηθέντος, ὅπως ἂν καὶ φωνηθῇ, εἴτε βαρβάρως εἴτε Ἑλληνικῶς εἴτε κυνικῶς ἢ βοϊκῶς, λόγου γε ὄντος μέτοχα τὰ ζῷα τὰ φωνητικά, τῶν μὲν ἀνθρώπων κατὰ νόμους τοὺς ἀνθρωπείους φθεγγομένων, τῶν δὲ ζῴων κατὰ νόμους οὓς παρὰ τῶν θεῶν καὶ τῆς

arisen. Everyone else is ordinary.[6] Yes, some people are making moral progress while others gush with ordinariness, but all of them, since they are human beings, still possess *logos*. It is because they are seduced by self-interest that the Stoics say that all the other animals without exception lack *logos*.[7] . . . But if one must speak the truth, not only is *logos* to be observed in all animals generally; in many of them it has the capacity to reach completeness.

Given that there are two kinds of *logos*, one that operates in expression and one that resides in one's disposition, let us begin with the expressive kind, which is based on sound. If indeed expressive *logos* is sound signifying via the tongue experiences that take place inside, in one's soul (and this is a universal definition that is not attached to a particular school but is simply part and parcel of the concept of *logos*), what aspect of that is lacking in animals that speak?[8] Why should an animal not have first thought about whatever it's experiencing before uttering what it's about to say? (By "thought" here I mean what is being voiced silently in the soul.) Whatever is voiced by the tongue, therefore, is *logos*, and animals that make sounds possess it. It doesn't matter if the

φύσεως εἴληχεν ἕκαστον. εἰ δὲ μὴ ἡμεῖς ξυνίεμεν, τί τοῦτο; οὐδὲ γὰρ τῆς Ἰνδῶν οἱ Ἕλληνες οὐδὲ τῆς Σκυθῶν ἢ Θρᾳκῶν ἢ Σύρων οἱ ἐν τῇ Ἀττικῇ τραφέντες· ἀλλ' ἴσα κλαγγῇ γεράνων ὁ τῶν ἑτέρων τοῖς ἑτέροις ἦχος προσπίπτει. καίτοι ἐγγράμματος τοῖς ἑτέροις ἡ αὐτῶν καὶ ἔναρθρος, ὡς καὶ ἡμῖν ἡ ἡμετέρα· ἄναρθρος δὲ καὶ ἀγράμματος ἡ τῶν Σύρων φέρε εἰπεῖν ἢ τῶν Περσῶν, ὡς καὶ πᾶσιν ἡ τῶν ζῴων. καθάπερ γὰρ ἡμεῖς ψόφου μόνου ἀντιλαμβανόμεθα καὶ ἤχου, ἀξύνετοι ὄντες τῆς [φέρε] Σκυθῶν ὁμιλίας, καὶ κλαγγάζειν δοκοῦσιν καὶ μηδὲν διαρθροῦν, ἀλλ' ἑνὶ ψόφῳ χρῆσθαι μακροτέρῳ ἢ βραχυτέρῳ, τὸ παρηλλαγμένον δὲ αὐτοῦ εἰς σημασίαν οὐδαμῶς προσπίπτει, ἐκείνοις δὲ εὐσύνετος ἡ φθέγξις καὶ πολὺ τὸ διάφορον ἔχουσα, καθάπερ ἡμῖν ἡ συνήθης· οὕτως καὶ ἐπὶ τῶν ζῴων ἡ ξύνεσις μὲν ἐκείνοις κατὰ γένος ἰδίως προσπίπτει, ἡμῖν δὲ ὁ ψόφος μόνος ἐξάκουστος, τῆς σημασίας ἐκλειπούσης, διὰ τὸ μηδένα διδαχθέντα τὴν ἡμετέραν διδάξαι ἡμᾶς διὰ τῆς ἡμετέρας τὴν ἑρμηνείαν τῶν λεγομένων παρὰ τοῖς ζῴοις. καίτοι εἰ δεῖ πιστεύειν τοῖς παλαιοῖς καὶ τοῖς ἐφ' ἡμῶν καὶ τῶν πατέρων γεγονόσιν, εἰσὶν οἳ λέγονται ἐπακοῦσαι καὶ

sound is expressed in the manner of a non-Greek, a Greek, a dog, or a cow. Humans make sounds according to human conventions, animals according to conventions allotted by the gods and by Nature to each one. If we do not understand them, so what? Greeks don't understand the sounds made by Indians. Those reared on the sounds of Attic Greek do not understand the sounds made by Scythians, Thracians, or Syrians. The sound that each one makes falls on the ears of the other like the whooping of cranes. Even though their sound making is comprehensible in writing and by oral articulation for them, as ours is for us, Syrian or Persian sounds, say, are *not* comprehensible to us, either orally or in writing, just as the sound making of animals is incomprehensible to us all.[9] We perceive only noise and sound, since we lack understanding of, say, the conversation of Scythians, who seem to us to cackle and to articulate nothing. To us it's just noises they make, sometimes long, sometimes short, but the modulations produce no meaning whatsoever. And yet their manner of speaking is easy for them to understand and the sounds very much distinguishable, just as our accustomed speech is to us. Likewise, in the case of animals,

σύνεσιν ἔχειν τῆς τῶν ζῴων φθέγξεως· ὡς ἐπὶ μὲν
τῶν παλαιῶν ὁ Μελάμπους καὶ ὁ Τειρεσίας καὶ οἱ
τοιοῦτοι, οὐ πρὸ πολλοῦ δὲ Ἀπολλώνιος ὁ Τυανεύς,
ἐφ᾽ οὗ καὶ λέγεται, ὅτι τοῖς ἑταίροις συνόντος,
χελιδόνος ἐπιπτάσης καὶ φθεγγομένης, εἶπεν
ὅτι μηνύει ἡ χελιδὼν ταῖς ἄλλαις ὄνον πρὸ τοῦ
ἄστεως πεπτωκέναι σίτου βαστάζοντα φορτίον, ὃ
δὴ κεχύσθαι εἰς τὴν γῆν τοῦ ἀχθοφοροῦντος πε-
πτωκότος. ἑταῖρος δὲ ἡμῶν ἐξηγεῖτό τις, οἰκέτου
εὐτυχῆσαι παιδός, ὃς πάντα ξυνίει τὰ φθέγματα
τῶν ὀρνίθων, καὶ ἦν πάντα μαντικὰ καὶ τοῦ μετ᾽
ὀλίγον μέλλοντος ἀγγελτικά· ἀφαιρεθῆναι δὲ τὴν
σύνεσιν, τῆς μητρὸς εὐλαβηθείσης μὴ δῶρον αὐτὸν
βασιλεῖ πέμψειεν, καὶ καθεύδοντος εἰς τὰ ὦτα
ἐνουρησάσης.

understanding comes to them in a way that is unique to each species. But for us it's only noise we hear, which lacks meaning because no one who's been taught our language has taught us to translate into Greek what is said by animals.

However, if we are to believe the ancients, and those who lived in our and our fathers' time, there are those who are said to be able to hear and understand the speech of animals. Among the ancients, there was Melampus, and Tiresias, and such like, and, not long ago, Apollonius of Tyana, who, when a swallow flew across the sky and began chirping, is reported to have said in the presence of his disciples: "The swallow is signifying to the other swallows that a donkey carrying a load of grain has taken a tumble outside town and the grain he was carrying has spilled on the ground."[10] A friend of mine, too, used to go on and on about how lucky he was to have an enslaved boy who understood all the utterances of birds, all of which were prophecies announcing what soon would happen, though he lost this understanding because his mother was concerned that he'd be sent to the emperor as a gift and so she urinated in his ears while he was sleeping.

4. ἀλλ᾽ ἵνα ταῦτα παρῶμεν διὰ τὸ ξύμφυτον ἡμῖν πάθος τῆς ἀπιστίας, ἀλλὰ τῶν γε ἐθνῶν τινὰ εἰς ἔτι καὶ νῦν ὅπως ξυγγένειαν ἔχει πρός τινων ζῴων σύνεσιν τῆς φθέγξεως, οὐδεὶς οἶμαι ἠγνόηκεν. Ἄραβες μὲν κοράκων ἀκούουσιν, Τυρρηνοὶ δ᾽ ἀετῶν· τάχα δ᾽ ἂν καὶ ἡμεῖς καὶ πάντες ἄνθρωποι συνετοὶ ἦμεν πάντων τῶν ζῴων, εἰ καὶ ἡμῶν τὰ ὦτα δράκων ἔνιψε. δηλοῖ γε μὴν καὶ τὸ ποικίλον καὶ διάφορον τῆς φθέγξεως αὐτῶν τὸ σημαντικόν. ἄλλως γοῦν ἀκούεται ὅταν φοβῆται φθεγγόμενα, ἄλλως ὅταν καλῇ, ἄλλως ὅταν εἰς τροφὴν παρακαλῇ, ἄλλως ὅταν φιλοφρονῆται, ἄλλως ὅταν προκαλῆται εἰς μάχην· καὶ τοσοῦτόν ἐστι τὸ διάφορον, ὡς καὶ σφόδρα δυσπαρατήρητον τὴν παραλλαγὴν εἶναι διὰ τὸ πλῆθος καὶ τοῖς τὸν βίον εἰς ‹τὴν› τούτων τήρησιν καταθεμένοις. κορώνης γοῦν καὶ κόρακος οἰωνισταὶ ἄχρι τινὸς [πλήθους] τὸ διάφορον σημειωσάμενοι, τὸ λοιπὸν εἴασαν ὡς οὐκ ὂν ἀνθρώπῳ εὐπερίληπτον. ὅταν δὲ πρὸς ἄλληλα φθέγγηται φανερά τε καὶ εὔσημα, εἰ καὶ μὴ πᾶσιν ἡμῖν γνώριμα, φαίνηται δὲ καὶ ἡμᾶς μιμούμενα καὶ τὴν Ἑλλάδα γλῶτταν ἐκμανθάνοντα καὶ συνιέντα τῶν ἐφεστώτων, τίς οὕτως ἀναιδὴς ὡς μὴ συγχωρεῖν εἶναι λογικά, διότι αὐτὸς οὐ συνίησιν ὧν λέγουσιν; κόρακες γοῦν καὶ κίτται ἐριθακοί τε καὶ ψιττακοὶ ἀνθρώπους μιμοῦνται καὶ μέμνηνται

But let us put these reports aside, since our natural inclination is to disbelieve them. On the other hand, no one, I think, is unaware that some peoples even today do in fact have a kind of affinity for understanding the speech of certain animals. Arabs, for example, can hear ravens, Etruscans eagles. Indeed, perhaps all of us humans would understand all animals if a snake had cleaned out our ears, too.[11] Certainly, at any rate, the complexity and variety of their utterance shows that it has meaning. Indeed, animals make different sounds for when they are afraid, when they call out, when they are asking for food, when they are being friendly, and when they're challenging to a fight. The variety is so great, in fact, that it is difficult to distinguish the variations, even for those who have dedicated their lives to observing animals, because there are so many. Bird augurs have identified the meaning of the different calls of crows and ravens—but only up to a certain number. They have relegated the rest as being too difficult for a human to comprehend.

Given that animals talk to one another distinctly and meaningfully, even if they are unintelligible to us, and can even be observed to mimic

ὧν ἂν ἀκούσωσιν καὶ διδασκόμενοι ὑπακούουσι
τῷ διδάσκοντι, καὶ πολλοί γε ἐμήνυσαν δι' ὧν ἐδι-
δάχθησαν καὶ τοὺς ἁμαρτάνοντας κατὰ τὸν οἶκον.
ἡ δ' Ἰνδικὴ ὕαινα, ἣν κοροκότταν οἱ ἐπιχώ- ριοι
καλοῦσι, καὶ ἄνευ διδασκάλου οὕτω φθέγγεται
ἀνθρωπικῶς, ὡς καὶ ἐπιφοιτᾶν ταῖς οἰκίαις καὶ καλεῖν ὃν <ἂν> ἴδῃ εὐχείρωτον αὐτῇ, καὶ μιμεῖταί γε
τοῦ φιλτάτου καὶ ᾧ ἂν πάντως ὑπακούσειεν ὁ κλη-
θεὶς τὸ φθέγμα· ὡς καίπερ εἰδότας τοὺς Ἰνδοὺς διὰ
τῆς ὁμοιότητος ἐξαπατᾶσθαι καὶ ἀναλίσκεσθαι

ἐξιόντας τε καὶ πρὸς τὸ φθέγμα ὑπακούοντας.
εἰ δὲ μὴ πάντα μιμητικὰ μηδὲ πάντα εὐμαθῆ τῆς
ἡμετέρας, τί τοῦτο; οὐδὲ γὰρ ἄνθρωπος πᾶς εὐμα-
θὴς ἢ μιμητικὸς οὐχ ὅτι τῆς τῶν ζῴων, ἀλλ' οὐδὲ
πέντε που διαλέκτων τῶν παρ' ἀνθρώποις. τινὰ δὲ
καὶ τῷ μὴ διδάσκεσθαι ἴσως οὐ φθέγγεται ἢ καὶ τῷ
ὑπὸ τῶν ὀργάνων τῶν τῆς φωνῆς ἐμποδίζεσθαι.

us and learn Greek and understand their owners, who would be so arrogant as to deny that they possess *logos*, just because he himself doesn't understand what they're saying? Ravens, magpies, robins, and parrots imitate humans. They remember what they hear, and, when they're trained, obey the person who teaches them. Indeed, many birds, because of what they've been taught, have informed on people misbehaving in the household. The Indian hyena, which the locals call a *corocotta*, speaks in so human a way, even without a trainer, that she prowls about houses, summoning whomever she thinks would be easy prey by mimicking that person's best friend's voice—the sound to which the friend would especially respond when called. Even though the Indians are aware of this, they are still fooled by the similarity, respond to the voice, then go out and get eaten anyway.

And what does it matter anyhow if not all animals imitate or comprehend our speech? Not every person can imitate or comprehend the speech of animals either. And a person, I'd venture to guess, can hardly learn five dialects of *human* speech. Maybe some animals don't talk because they've not been taught to or are prevented

ἡμεῖς γοῦν κατὰ Καρχηδόνα, πέρδικος ἐπιπτάντος
ἡμέρου, τρέφοντες τοῦτον, τοῦ χρόνου προϊόντος
καὶ τῆς συνηθείας εἰς πολλὴν ἡμερότητα αὐτὸν με-
ταβαλούσης, οὐ μόνον σαίνοντος καὶ θεραπεύο-
ντος ᾐσθόμεθα καὶ προσπαίζοντος, ἀλλ' ἤδη καὶ
ἀντιφθεγγομένου πρὸς τὸ ἡμέτερον φθέγμα καὶ
καθ' ὅσον ἦν δυνατὸν ἀποκρινομένου, ἀλλοίως ἢ
καλεῖν ἀλλήλους εἰώθασιν οἱ πέρδικες. οὔκουν σι-
ωπῶντος, φθεγξαμένου δ' ἀντεφθέγξατο μόνον.

5. ἱστορεῖται δὲ καὶ τῶν ἀφθόγγων <τινὰ> οὕτως
ἑτοίμως ὑπακούειν τοῖς δεσπόταις, ὡς οὐκ <ἂν>
ἄνθρωπος τῶν συνήθων. ἡ γοῦν Κράσσου τοῦ Ῥω-
μαϊκοῦ μύραινα ὀνομαστὶ καλουμένη προσῄει τῷ
Κράσσῳ, ὃν καὶ οὕτως διέθηκεν, ὡς πενθῆσαι
ἀποθανοῦσαν, τριῶν τέκνων ἀποβολὴν πρότερον
μετρίως ἐνεγκόντα. καὶ ἐγχέλεις δὲ πολλοὶ ἱστό-
ρησαν τὰς ἐν Ἀρεθούσῃ καὶ σαπέρδας τοὺς περὶ
Μαίανδρον ὑπακούοντας τοῖς καλοῦσιν. οὔκουν
φαντασία ἡ αὐτὴ <τῇ> τοῦ λέγοντος, ἐάν τε ἐπὶ
γλῶτταν ἐξικνῆται ἐάν τε μή. πῶς οὖν οὐκ ἄγνω-
μον μόνην λόγον τὴν ἀνθρώπου φωνὴν λέγειν, ὅτι
ἡμῖν ξυνετή, τὴν δὲ τῶν ἄλλων ζῴων παραιτεῖσθαι;
ὅμοιον γὰρ ὡς εἰ κόρακες τὴν σφῶν μόνην ἠξίουν

from speaking by their vocal organs. I had a partridge once at Carthage, for example, a tame one that I had reared. As time went on and it became even tamer from our acquaintance, it would fly over to me, and I noticed it would coo greetings to me, look after me, and would even be playful. What is more, it would speak back in response to my speech, and, as best it could, would reply to me, albeit differently from how partridges ordinarily call to one another. When I was silent, however, it said nothing; it spoke only in reply when I had said something.

It's been documented that even some voiceless animals respond to their masters more readily than even a human companion would. An eel belonging to the Roman Crassus, for example, would come to him when called by its name. This had such an effect on Crassus that when the eel died, he mourned it, though when three of his own children had died earlier, he bore that loss with equanimity.[12] Many people report that eels in the spring at Arethusa and the perch in the Maeander River respond when they are called. Clearly, the capacity to formulate a mental image is the same here as in the case of one who can speak, whether it reaches the tongue or not.[13]

εἶναι φωνήν, ἡμᾶς δ᾽ εἶναι ἀλόγους, διότι οὐκ
αὐτοῖς εὔσημα φθεγγόμεθα· ἢ οἱ Ἀττικοὶ εἰ μόνην
τὴν Ἀτθίδα ἔλεγον φωνήν, τοὺς δὲ ἄλλους ἀλόγους
ἡγοῦντο τοὺς λέξεως Ἀττικῆς ἀμοιροῦντας. καίτοι
θᾶττον ἂν κόρακος ξύνεσιν λάβοι ὁ Ἀττικὸς ἢ
Σύρου ἢ Πέρσου συρίζοντος καὶ περσίζοντος. ἀλλὰ
μήποτε ἄτοπον ἐκ τῆς εὐσυνέτου φθέγξεως ἢ μὴ ἢ
τῆς σιγῆς καὶ φωνῆς τὸ λογικὸν κρίνειν καὶ τὸ
ἄλογον· οὕτως γὰρ καὶ τὸν ἐπὶ πᾶσι θεὸν καὶ τοὺς
ἄλλους τῷ μὴ φθέγγεσθαι φαίη ἄν τις μὴ εἶναι λο-
γικούς. ἀλλ᾽ οἵ γε θεοὶ σιγῶντες μηνύουσι. . . . καὶ
μὴν καὶ ἡμῶν οἱ παρατηροῦντες καὶ οἱ σύντροφοι
γιγνώσκουσιν αὐτῶν τὰ φθέγματα. ὁ γοῦν κυνηγέτης ἀπὸ τῆς ὑποκρίσεως ᾔσθετο τοῦ κυνὸς
ὑλακτοῦντος νῦν μὲν ὅτι ζητεῖ τὸν λαγῶν, νῦν δὲ
ὅτι εὗρεν, νῦν δὲ ὅτι διώκει, νῦν δὲ ὅτι ἔλαβεν,
καὶ πλανωμένου ὅτι πλανᾶται. καὶ ὁ βουκόλος
οἶδεν ὅτι ἡ βοῦς πεινῇ ἢ διψῇ ἢ κέκμηκεν ἢ ὀργᾷ ἢ
τὸν μόσχον ζητεῖ· καὶ λέων βρυχώμενος δηλοῖ ὅτι
ἀπειλεῖ, καὶ λύκος ὠρυόμενος ὅτι κακῶς πράσσει,
καὶ ὄϊες βληχώμεναι οὐκ ἔλαθον τὸν ποιμένα
ὅτου δέονται.

How then can it not be senseless to ascribe *logos* only to human speech, because it's intelligible to us, and to discount the speech of the other animals? That would be like crows saying that theirs is the only language and that *we* lack *logos* because we say things that are not easy for them to understand, or if inhabitants of Attica were to say that Attic is the only language and considered all others who don't speak the Attic dialect to lack *logos*. And yet the Attic speaker would sooner comprehend a crow than he would a Syrian speaking Syrian or a Persian speaking Persian. It is certainly out of place to judge something to be either with or without *logos* based on whether its speech is easy to understand, or, for that matter, by its sound or its silence. According to that logic, one could argue that the God who presides over all and the other gods, too, lack *logos* because they don't speak to us, since gods communicate to us in silence. . . .

In addition, those of us who observe animals and live alongside them recognize the sounds they make. The hunter, for example, perceives from the replies of his dog when he is barking, first that he is searching for a rabbit, now that he's found it, then that he's on the chase, then that he's caught

6. . . . εἰ μέντοι πιστεύειν δεῖ Ἀριστοτέλει, καὶ δι-
δάσκοντα ὤφθη οὐ μόνον τῶν ἄλλων τι ποιεῖν τὰ
τέκνα τὰ ζῷα, ἀλλὰ καὶ φθέγγεσθαι, ὡς ἀηδὼν τὸν
νεοττὸν ᾄδειν. καὶ ὡς αὐτός γε φησίν, πολλὰ μὲν
παρ᾽ ἀλλήλων μανθάνει ζῷα, πολλὰ δὲ καὶ παρ᾽ ἀνθρώπων, καὶ πᾶς αὐτῷ ἀληθεύοντι μαρτυρεῖ, πᾶς
μὲν πωλοδάμνης, πᾶς δὲ ἱπποκόμος τε καὶ ἱππεὺς
καὶ ἡνίοχος, πᾶς δὲ κυνηγέτης τε καὶ ἐλεφαντιστὴς
καὶ βουκόλος καὶ οἱ τῶν θηρίων διδάσκαλοι οἵ τε
τῶν ὀρνίθων πάντες. ἀλλ᾽ ὁ μὲν εὐγνώμων καὶ
ἐκ τούτων μεταδίδωσι συνέσεως τοῖς ζῴοις, ὁ δὲ
ἀγνώμων καὶ ἀνιστόρητος αὐτῶν φέρεται συνερ-
γῶν αὐτοῦ τῇ εἰς αὐτὰ πλεονεξίᾳ. καὶ πῶς γὰρ οὐκ
ἔμελλεν κακολογήσειν καὶ διαβαλεῖν ἃ κατακόπτειν ὡς λίθον προῄρηται. . . .

it, or if he's lost his way, the hunter knows that too. The cowherd knows if his cow is hungry, or thirsty, or tired, or in heat, or is looking for her calf. A lion, too, shows by his roaring that he poses a threat, a wolf by his howling that he's in a poor way; and when sheep bleat, the shepherd understands what they need. . . .

If Aristotle is to be believed, animals have been observed to teach their young not only to do things, but also to speak, as a nightingale teaches her chick to sing. And, he says, animals learn many things from one another and many things from humans, too. Indeed, everyone confirms that Aristotle's testimony is true: every horse breaker, every groom, every equestrian and charioteer, as well as every hunter, mahout, cowherd, and everyone who trains wild beasts and birds. A sensible person, then, based just on this evidence, grants animals a share in intelligence. It's the ignorant person who has done no research about animals that is misguided, aided in this error by his own greediness with respect to them.[14] How could he *not* inevitably slander and abuse creatures he's already chosen in advance to carve up as if they were stone? . . .

7. δεικτέον δὲ καὶ τὸν ἐντὸς αὐτῶν καὶ ἐνδιάθε-
τον. φαίνεται δὲ ἡ παραλλαγή, ὡς φησί που καὶ
Ἀριστοτέλης, οὐκ οὐσίᾳ διαλλάττουσα, ἀλλ᾽ ἐν τῷ
μᾶλλον καὶ ἧττον θεωρουμένη· καθάπερ πολλοὶ
οἴονται καὶ τὴν θεῶν πρὸς ἡμᾶς ἐξηλλάχθαι, οὐ
κατ᾽ οὐσίαν οὔσης τῆς διαφορᾶς ταύτης, ἀλλὰ κατὰ
τὸ ἀκριβὲς ἢ μὴ τοῦ λόγου. καὶ ὅτι μὲν ἄχρι γε αἰσθήσεως τῆς τε ἄλλης ὀργανώσεως τῆς τε κατὰ τὰ
αἰσθητήρια καὶ τῆς κατὰ σάρκα ὁμοίως ἡμῖν διά-
κειται, πᾶς σχεδὸν συγκεχώρηκεν. καὶ γὰρ οὐ
μόνον τῶν κατὰ φύσιν παθῶν τε καὶ κινημάτων τῶν
διὰ τούτων ὁμοίως ἡμῖν κεκοινώνηκεν, ἀλλ᾽ ἤδη καὶ
τῶν παρὰ φύσιν καὶ νοσωδῶν ἐν αὐτοῖς θεωρου-
μένων. οὐκ ἂν δέ τις εὖ φρονῶν διὰ τὸ ἐξηλλαγμέ-
νον τῆς ἕξεως τοῦ σώματος ἄδεκτα λογικῆς εἴποι
διαθέσεως, ὁρῶν καὶ ἐπ᾽ ἀνθρώπων πολλὴν τὴν
παραλλαγὴν τῆς ἕξεως κατά τε γένη καὶ ἔθνη, καὶ
ὅμως λογικοὺς συγχωρῶν πάντας. ὄνος μέν γε κα-
τάρρῳ ἁλίσκεται, κἂν εἰς πνεύμονα αὐτῷ ῥυῇ τὸ
νόσημα, ἀποθνήσκει ὥσπερ ἄνθρωπος· ἵππος δὲ
καὶ ἔμπυος γίνεται καὶ φθίνει, ὥσπερ ἄνθρωπος,
καὶ τέτανος λαμβάνει ἵππον καὶ ποδάγρα καὶ πυ-
ρετὸς καὶ λύσσα, ὁπότε καὶ κατωπιᾶν λέγεται. καὶ
ἡ κύουσα ἵππος, ἐπειδὰν ὀσφρήσηται λύχνου ἀπε-
σβεσμένου, ἀμβλίσκει ὡς ἄνθρωπος. πυρέττει δὲ
καὶ βοῦς καὶ μαίνεται, καθάπερ καὶ ὁ κάμηλος.

Animals' internal *logos*, the one that resides in them, can also be demonstrated. It's clear that variation, as Aristotle says somewhere, is not to be seen as a difference in essence but as a question of more and less, just as many people think that while there is a big difference between the gods and us, that difference is not one of essence but of degree, measured by the exactness, or not, of the *logos* each possesses. That animals are like us, at least as far as perception and physical constitution are concerned—that is, with respect to sense organs and flesh—almost everyone agrees. They partake like us not only in experiences of natural processes and the movements thus produced, but also, indeed, in unnatural diseases that can be observed arising in them.[15] No one who is thinking straight could say that animals are incapable of a rational disposition[16] because of some fundamental difference in bodily constitution when he sees that even among humans, too, there is great variation of constitution according to ethnicity and race, and yet still agree that all *humans* are rational. A donkey, for example, can catch a cold and, if the malady runs down into its lungs, die, just like a human. A horse, likewise, gets abscesses and wasting disease just like a human, and tetanus

κορώνη δὲ ψωριᾷ καὶ λεπριᾷ, <ὥσπερ> καὶ κύων·
οὗτος μέν γε καὶ ποδαγριᾷ καὶ λυσσᾷ. ὗς δὲ βραγχᾷ,
καὶ ἔτι μᾶλλον κύων, καὶ τὸ πάθος ἐν ἀνθρώπῳ ἀπὸ
τοῦ κυνὸς κυνάγχη κέκληται. καὶ ταῦτα <μὲν>
γνώριμα, ἐπεὶ σύννομα ταῦτα ἡμῖν τὰ ζῷα, τῶν δὲ
ἄλλων ἐσμὲν ἄπειροι διὰ τὸ ἀσύνηθες. καὶ εὐνου-
χιζόμενα δὲ μαλακίζεται· οἱ μέν γε ἀλεκτρυόνες
οὐδὲ ᾄδουσιν ἔτι, ἀλλὰ τὴν φωνὴν ἐπὶ τὸ θῆλυ με-
ταβάλλουσιν ὥσπερ ἄνθρωποι, βοός τε κέρατα καὶ
φωνὴν οὐκ ἔστι διαγνῶναι τομίου καὶ θήλεος· οἱ
δὲ ἔλαφοι οὐκέτι ἀποβάλλουσι τὰ κέρατα, ἀλλὰ
συνέχουσιν, ὡς εὐνοῦχοι τὰς τρίχας, μὴ ἔχοντες δὲ
οὐ φύουσιν, ὥσπερ οἱ πρὶν πώγωνα φῦσαι ἐκτμη-
θέντες. οὕτως σχεδὸν ἁπάντων τὰ σώματα ὁμοίως
τοῖς ἡμετέροις κατὰ τὰ πάθη.

8. τά γε μὴν τῆς ψυχῆς πάθη ὅρα εἰ μὴ πάντα
ὅμοια· καὶ πρῶτά γε τὴν αἴσθησιν. οὐ γὰρ δὴ

and gout and fevers and rabies and sometimes, too, is said to "cast down its eyes."[17] A pregnant mare, like a human, miscarries if she gets a whiff of a lamp that's been snuffed out.[18] Cows get fevers and go berserk, as do camels. A crow gets the mange and leprosy, as does a dog. (A dog also gets gout and rabies.) A pig becomes hoarse—a dog even more so—and this affliction in a human is in fact called "dog throttle" after the dog. And these are the known cases, since these animals share our habitat; about other animals we are ignorant because of our lack of familiarity with them. When castrated, animals, too, become soft: Roosters no longer crow, but their voice is feminized, just as with humans, and it's impossible to tell the difference between the horns and the voice of a castrated bull and a female cow. Gelded stags no longer shed their antlers but retain them, just as eunuchs do their hair; whereas if they didn't have antlers before, they don't grow them, just as humans who have been castrated before they'd grown beards remain beardless.[19] Thus, the bodies of almost all animals are akin to ours when it comes to morbidity.[20]

When it comes to the experiences of the soul, too, see if these are not also similar. Consider, for

ἀνθρώπου μὲν ἡ γεῦσις χυμῶν, ἡ δὲ ὄψις χροιῶν, ἢ
ὀσμῶν ἡ ὄσφρησις ἀντιλαμβάνεται, ἢ ψόφων
ἡ ἀκοή, ἢ θερμῶν ἢ ψυχρῶν ἡ ἁφὴ ἢ τῶν ἄλλων
ἁπτῶν, οὐχὶ δὲ καὶ τῶν ζῴων ἁπάντων ὁμοίως.
οὐδὲ ταύτης μὲν ἀφήρηται τὰ ζῷα διὰ τὸ μὴ εἶναι
ἄνθρωποι, λογικῆς δὲ ἀμοιροῦσι διὰ τοῦτο· ἐπεὶ
οὕτω γε καὶ οἱ θεοὶ διὰ τὸ μὴ εἶναι ἄνθρωποι λογικῆς στερήσονται, ἢ ἡμεῖς, εἴπερ οἱ θεοὶ λογικοί. αἰσθήσεως μέν γε καὶ πλεονεκτεῖν ἔοικεν μᾶλλον τὰ
ζῷα. τίς μὲν γὰρ ἀνθρώπων τοσοῦτον βλέπει [οὐδὲ
γὰρ ὁ μυθευόμενος Λυγκεύς] ὅσον ὁ δράκων; ὅθεν
καὶ τὸ βλέπειν δρακεῖν λέγουσιν οἱ ποιηταί· τὸν δὲ
ἀετὸν 'καὶ ὑψόθ᾽ ἐόντα οὐκ ἔλαθε πτώξ'. τίς δὲ ὀξυ-
ηκοώτερος γεράνων, αἳ ἀπὸ τοσούτων ἀκούουσιν
ὅπως οὐδὲ ἀνθρώπων τις ὁρᾷ τῇ μὲν γὰρ ὀσφρή-
σει τοσούτῳ πλεονεκτεῖ σχεδὸν πάντα τὰ ζῷα, ὡς
ἐκείνοις προσπίπτειν τὰ ἡμᾶς λανθάνοντα, καὶ
κατὰ γένος ἐπιγινώσκειν ἕκαστον ἤδη καὶ ἐξ ἴχνους
ὀσφραινόμενα. οἱ δὲ ἄνθρωποι ἡγεμόσι κυσὶ χρῶ-
νται, εἰ δεῖ ἐλθεῖν ἐπὶ σῦν ἢ ἔλαφον· καὶ ἡμῶν μὲν
ὀψὲ ἡ τοῦ ἀέρος κατάστασις ἅπτεται, τῶν δὲ ἄλλων
ζῴων εὐθύς, ὡς τούτοις τεκμηρίοις χρῆσθαι τοῦ
μέλλοντος. τὴν δὲ τῶν χυμῶν διάκρισιν οὕτως
οἶδεν, ὡς ἐξακριβοῦν καὶ τὰ νοσερὰ καὶ τὰ ὑγιεινὰ
καὶ τὰ δηλητήρια, ὡς οὐδὲ ἀνθρώπων οἱ ἰατροί.
φρονιμώτερα δὲ φησιν ὁ Ἀριστοτέλης εἶναι τὰ

example, perception. To taste flavors, to see colors, to have a sense of smell that perceives scents do not belong to humans alone, nor does the hearing of noises, nor the sense of touch to feel hot and cold and other tactile qualities. These belong to all animals as well. Animals, then, are not deprived of perception because they are not human and do not lack rationality because of that fact either. If that were the case, the gods are to be robbed of rationality for not being human—or we are, if the gods are rational. As far as perception is concerned, animals seem rather to outdo us. What human being has such keen vision as a snake [*drakōn*]? Not even the legendary Lynceus![21] That is why the poets use the verb *drakein* for "seeing." And so, too,

> the hare does not escape the high-flying
> eagle.[22]

Who has keener hearing than cranes? They can hear across greater distances than a human being can even see. And when it comes to the sense of smell, nearly all animals outstrip us: They pick up on scents of which we are wholly unaware, and they recognize one another's species just by

εὐαισθητότερα. σωμάτων δὲ παραλλαγαὶ εὐπαθῆ μὲν ἢ δυσπαθῆ ποιῆσαι δύνανται, καὶ μᾶλλον ἢ ἧττον πρόχειρον ἔχειν τὸν λόγον, κατ' οὐσίαν δὲ τὴν ψυχὴν ἐξαλλάττειν οὐ δύνανται, ὅπου γε οὐδὲ τὰς αἰσθήσεις οὐδὲ τὰ πάθη ἔτρεψαν, οὐδὲ τέλεον ἐκβεβηκυίας ἐποίησαν. ἐν οὖν τῷ μᾶλλον καὶ ἧττον ἡ διαφορὰ συγχωρείσθω, οὐκ ἐν τῇ τελείᾳ στερή-σει· οὐδ' ἐν τῷ καθάπαξ τὸ μὲν ἔχειν, τὸ δὲ μή· ἀλλ' ὡς ἐν ἑνὶ γένει τὸ μὲν ὑγιεινότερον σῶμά ἐστιν, τὸ δὲ ἧττον, καὶ ἐπὶ νόσου ὁμοίως πολὺ τὸ διάφορον, ἔν τε εὐφυΐαις καὶ ἀφυΐαις, οὕτω καὶ ἐν ψυχαῖς ἡ μὲν ἀγαθή, ἡ δὲ φαύλη· καὶ τῶν φαύλων ἡ μὲν μᾶλλον, ἡ δὲ ἧττον· καὶ τῶν ἀγαθῶν οὐχ ἡ αὐτὴ ἰσότης, οὐδὲ ὁμοίως Σωκράτης ἀγαθὸς καὶ Ἀρι-στοτέλης καὶ Πλάτων, οὐδ' ἐν ὁμοδόξοις ἡ ταυτό-της. οὐ τοίνυν οὐδ' εἰ μᾶλλον ἡμεῖς νοοῦμεν ἢ τὰ ζῷα, διὰ τοῦτο ἀφαιρετέον τῶν ζῴων τὸ νοεῖν, ὥσπερ οὐδὲ τὸ πέτεσθαι τοὺς πέρδικας, ὅτι μᾶλλον αὐτῶν <οἱ> ἱέρακες πέτονται, οὐδὲ τοὺς ἄλλους ἱέρακας, ὅτι καὶ τούτων καὶ τῶν ἄλλων ἁπάντων ὁ φασσοφόνος. . . .

sniffing their tracks. Humans use dogs as guides if they need to follow the trail of a wild boar or a deer. We are late to ascertain weather conditions, whereas for all other animals this is instantaneous—so much so that we use them as indicators of what's to come. Animals know how to differentiate flavors so well that they discriminate precisely what is sickening, what is healthy, and what will outright kill them. Not even human doctors can do that. Aristotle says that animals with keener senses are more sagacious. Bodily variations make animals either readily or less readily susceptible to experiences and thus more or less capable of utilizing reason. But variations cannot make an animal's soul fundamentally different in essence, at least in cases where variation has not changed the experiences and perceptions or made them disappear entirely. Let us agree, therefore, that the difference is a question of more and less and not complete deprivation. Nor is it a once-and-for-all question of have or have not. Just as in a single species one body is healthier, another less so—and there is a big difference regarding disease, too, in the case of both good and poor physical conditions—so also in souls: one is good, another is bad. And among the bad, too, one is

9. ὅτι τοίνυν καὶ λογικὴ ἐν αὐτοῖς ἔστιν καὶ οὐκ ἀφῄρηται φρονήσεως ἐπιδεικτέον. πρῶτον μὲν ἕκαστον οἶδεν εἴτε ἀσθενές ἐστιν εἴτε ἰσχυρόν, καὶ τὰ μὲν φυλάττεται, τοῖς δὲ χρῆται, ὡς πάρδαλις μὲν ὀδοῦσιν, ὄνυξι δὲ λέων καὶ ὀδοῦσιν, ἵππος δὲ ὁπλῇ καὶ βοῦς κέρασιν, καὶ ἀλεκτρυὼν μὲν πλήκτρῳ, σκορπίος δὲ κέντρῳ· οἱ δ' ἐν Αἰγύπτῳ ὄφεις πτύσματι [ὅθεν καὶ πτυάδες καλοῦνται] ἐκτυφλοῦσι τὰς ὄψεις τῶν ἐπιόντων, ἄλλο δὲ ἄλλῳ χρῆται, σῷζον ἑαυτὸ ἕκαστον. πάλιν τὰ μὲν ἐκποδὼν νέμεται τῶν ἀνθρώπων, ὅσα ἰσχυρά· τὰ δὲ ἀγεννῆ ἐκποδὼν μὲν τῶν ἰσχυροτέρων θηρίων, τοὔμπαλιν δὲ μετὰ τῶν ἀνθρώπων· καὶ ἢ πορρωτέρω [μέν], ὡς στρουθοὶ ἐν ὀροφαῖς καὶ χελιδόνες, ἢ καὶ συνανθρωποῦντα, ὡς οἱ κύνες. ἀμείβει δὲ καὶ

more so, another less so. Even among the good there is not sameness: Socrates, Aristotle, and Plato are not all good in the same way. Even among people who hold the same opinions there's no identicalness. So even if we humans think more than animals do, that doesn't deprive them of thought altogether, in the same way that partridges are not deprived of flight because falcons fly more than partridges, and likewise falcons are not deprived because hawks fly more than falcons (and indeed more than all other birds). . . .

Now we must demonstrate that there is a rational soul in animals and that it doesn't lack the capacity for forming judgments. First, each animal knows where it is weak and where it is strong and is on its guard against its weakness while making use of its strength. A leopard uses its teeth, a lion its claws and teeth, a horse its hooves, and a bull its horns. A cockerel uses its spurs and a scorpion its sting. The snakes in Egypt use their spittle, and so are called "spitters" for this reason, blinding the eyes of those that attack them. Various animals use various means, each one to preserve itself. Moreover, strong animals keep themselves out of humans' way. Less endowed animals, in turn, keep away from the stronger

τόπους κατὰ τὰς ὥρας, καὶ πᾶν ὅσον τὸ πρὸς τὸ
συμφέρον οἶδεν. ὁμοίως δ' ἄν τις καὶ ἐπὶ ἰχθύων
ἴδοι τὸν τοιοῦτον λογισμὸν καὶ ἐπ' ὀρνίθων. . . .

10. ὁ δὲ φύσει λέγων αὐτοῖς προσεῖναι ταῦτα
ἀγνοεῖ λέγων ὅτι φύσει ἐστὶ λογικά, ἢ ὡς τοῦ λόγου
μὴ φύσει ἐν ἡμῖν συνισταμένου, καὶ τῆς τελειώ-
σεως μὴ καθὸ πεφύκαμεν τὴν αὔξησιν λαμβανού-
σης. τὸ μέν γε θεῖον οὐδὲ διὰ μαθήσεως λογικὸν
γέγονεν· οὐ γὰρ ἦν ὅτε ἦν ἄλογον, ἀλλ' ἅμα τε ἦν
καὶ λογικὸν ἦν, καὶ οὐ κεκώλυται εἶναι λογικόν, ὅτι
οὐ διὰ διδασκαλίας ἀνέλαβε τὸν λόγον. καίτοι ἐπὶ
τῶν ἄλλων ζῴων, καθάπερ ἐπὶ τῶν ἀνθρώπων, τὰ
μὲν πολλὰ ἐν αὐτοῖς ἡ φύσις ἐδίδαξεν, τὰ δὲ ἤδη
παρέσχε καὶ ἡ μάθησις· διδάσκονται δὲ τὰ μὲν ὑπ'
ἀλλήλων, τὰ δέ, ὡς ἔφαμεν, ὑπὸ ἀνθρώπων. καὶ
ἔχει γε μνήμην, ἥπερ εἰς ἀνάληψιν λογισμοῦ καὶ
φρονήσεως ἐτύγχανεν οὖσα κυριωτάτη. εἰσὶ δὲ
καὶ κακίαι ἄφθονοι ἐν αὐτοῖς, εἰ καὶ μὴ οὕτω κέχυ-
νται ὥσπερ ἐν ἀνθρώποις· ἔστιν γὰρ αὐτῶν ἡ κακία
κουφοτέρα τῆς ἀνθρώπων. αὐτίκα ἀνὴρ μὲν οἰκο-
δόμος οἰκίας θεμέλια οὐκ ἂν καταβάλοιτο μὴ

beasts and instead dwell among humans, albeit at a distance, like swallows and sparrows in the roof eaves, or they live in human company, as do dogs. Animals also change their location according to the season and have knowledge of everything that works to their advantage. No doubt, one would see similar reasoning exercised among fish and birds. . . .

The person who says animals possess these characteristics by nature is unaware that in so saying he is admitting that they are *rational* by nature—otherwise it would mean that reason is not lodged naturally *in us* either and that the growth to fullness of what we are by nature could not occur. What is divine, by contrast, has not become rational by learning. There was no moment that the divine was not rational. It was rational at its existence. Nor was the divine ever prevented from being rational, for it did not acquire its rationality through instruction. However, in the case of the other animals, just as with humans, Nature has taught much of what is in them and the learning process added much else. As we have said, animals learn some things from one another and other things from humans. They possess, in fact, *memory*, which is of chief importance in the

νήφων, οὐδὲ ναυπηγὸς νεὼς τρόπιν μὴ ὑγιαίνων, οὐδὲ γεωργὸς ἄμπελον φυτεύσαι μὴ πρὸς τοῦτο τὸν νοῦν ἔχων· παιδοποιοῦνται δὲ σχεδὸν πάντες μεθύοντες. ἀλλ᾽ οὐ τά γε ζῷα· ζῳογονεῖ δὲ τέκνων ἕνεκα, καὶ τὰ πλεῖστα, ὅταν ἐγκύμονα ποιήσῃ τὴν θήλειαν, οὔτε αὐτὰ ἐπιβαίνειν ἐπιχειρεῖ, οὔτε τὸ θῆλυ ἀνέχεται. ἡ δὲ ὕβρις ὅση ἐν τούτοις ἡ ἀνθρώπειος καὶ ἀκολασία δήλη. οἶδεν δὲ ἐπὶ τῶν ζῴων τὰς ὠδῖνας ὁ σύνοικος, καὶ συνωδίνει γε τὰ πολλά, ὥσπερ καὶ ἀλεκτρυόνες· τὰ δὲ καὶ συνεκλέπει, ὡς ταῖς περιστεραῖς οἱ ἄρρενες· καὶ τόπου προνοεῖ, οὗ μέλλουσι τίκτειν. καὶ γεννῆσαν ἕκαστον ἐκκαθαίρει τὸ γεννώμενον καὶ ἑαυτό. παρατηρήσας δ᾽ ἄν τις κατίδοι καὶ σὺν τάξει ἰόντα πάντα καὶ διαπαντῶντα μετὰ τοῦ σαίνειν τῷ τρέφοντι καὶ ἐπιγινώσκειν τὸν δεσπότην καὶ μηνύειν τὸν ἐπίβουλον.

acquisition of reasoning and judgment. There's also bad behavior and envy among animals, even if it isn't so widespread as it is among humans. And animal wrongdoing is anyhow far gentler than human wrongdoing. For example, a builder, should not lay down foundations for a house if he isn't sober. A shipwright should not fit the keel on a ship if he isn't in good health. A farmer shouldn't graft vines if his mind isn't on the job. And yet practically everyone procreates when drunk! Animals don't do this. They propagate for the sake of offspring, and in most cases, when the male has made the female pregnant, he does not try to mount her again, nor does the female allow it. How much wantonness and lack of restraint there is in these matters among humans is obvious. Among animals the male partner is cognizant of labor pains and oftentimes labors along with his mate, as, for example, with roosters. Some even help with hatching, as male pigeons do for the females. Animals think ahead about the place they'll give birth, and, once delivered, each one cleans off its offspring and itself. Anyone who has observed animals will have noticed that they all approach the human who feeds them in set order

11. τὰ δὲ συναγελαστικὰ ὅπως τηρεῖ τὸ δίκαιον τὸ πρὸς ἄλληλα, τίς ἀγνοεῖ; τοῦτο μὲν μυρμήκων ἔκαστον, τοῦτο δὲ καὶ μελιττῶν καὶ τῶν ὁμοίων. τίς δὲ σωφροσύνης φαττῶν πρὸς τοὺς συνοίκους, αἳ καὶ μοιχευθεῖσαι ἀναιροῦσιν εἰ λάβοιεν τὸν μοιχεύ- σαντα, ἢ τῆς τῶν πελαργῶν δικαιοσύνης πρὸς τοὺς τεκόντας ἀνήκοος. . . .

12. θαυμάσειε δ' ἄν τις τοὺς τὴν δικαιοσύνην ἐκ τοῦ λογικοῦ συνιστάντας καὶ τὰ μὴ κοινωνοῦντα τῶν ζῴων ἄγρια καὶ ἄδικα λέγοντας, μηκέτι δὲ ἄχρι τῶν κοινωνούντων τὴν δικαιοσύνην ἐκτείνοντας. καθάπερ γὰρ ἐπὶ τῶν ἀνθρώπων οἴχεται τὸ ζῆν ἀρ- θείσης τῆς κοινωνίας, οὕτω κἀκείνοις. ὄρνιθες γοῦν καὶ κύνες καὶ πολλὰ τῶν τετραπόδων, οἷον αἶγες, ἵπποι, πρόβατα, ὄνοι, ἡμίονοι, τῆς μετὰ ἀν- θρώπων κοινωνίας ἀφαιρεθέντα ἔρρει. καὶ ἡ δημι- ουργήσασα αὐτὰ φύσις ἐν χρείᾳ τῶν ἀνθρώπων κατέστησεν τούς τε ἀνθρώπους εἰς τὸ χρήζειν αὐτῶν, τὸ δίκαιον ἔμ- φυτον αὐτοῖς τε πρὸς ἡμᾶς καὶ ἡμῖν πρὸς αὐτὰ κατασκευάσασα. εἰ δέ τινα πρὸς ἀνθρώπους ἀγριαίνει, θαυμαστὸν οὐδέν· ἀληθὲς γὰρ ἦν τὸ τοῦ Ἀριστοτέλους, ὡς ἀφθονίαν

and mobs him with attention[23] and that they recognize their master and warn against a predator.

And who is ignorant of how animals that live in groups observe justice toward one another? Each ant does this, for example, as does each bee, and other creatures of that ilk. Who hasn't heard of the chastity that ringdoves display toward their mates, who, if they have been violated by another, kill the perpetrator if they catch him? And what about the justice that storks display toward their parents?[24] . . .

One might be surprised at people who base justice on reason and say that animals that form no part of society are wild and unjust and yet do not extend justice even to those animals that do form part of society. For just as life is ruined for human beings if society is removed, so too for animals. Birds and dogs and many four-footed animals like goats, horses, sheep, donkeys, and mules, if deprived of human society, perish. The nature that fashioned them brought it about that they need humans and humans need them and established thereby an innate justice principle for them toward us and for us toward them. If some animals are aggressive toward humans, that's no surprise. On this point Aristotle's observation is

εἰ τῆς τροφῆς πάντα ἐκέκτητο, οὔτ' ἂν πρὸς ἄλληλα οὔτε πρὸς ἀνθρώπους ἔσχεν ἂν ἀγρίως·
ταύτης γὰρ χάριν, καίτοι ἀναγκαίας καὶ εὐτελοῦς
οὔσης, αἵ τε ἔχθραι καὶ αἱ φιλίαι
    αὐτοῖς, καὶ τοῦ τόπου ἕνεκα. ἄνθρωποι δὲ εἰ
οὕτως εἰς στενὸν κομιδῇ κατεκέκλειντο ὡς τὰ ζῷα,
πόσῳ ἂν ἀγριώτεροι καὶ τῶν δοκούντων ἀγρίων
ἐγένοντο; διέδειξεν δὲ καὶ ὁ πόλεμος καὶ λιμός,
ὅπου οὐδὲ γεύσασθαι φείδονται ἀλλήλων· καὶ ἄνευ
γε πολέμου καὶ λιμοῦ τὰ σύντροφα καὶ ἥμερα τῶν
ζῴων κατεσθίουσιν.
    . . .

    18. . . . οὐ γὰρ καὶ πρὸς τὰ φυτὰ παρατενοῦμεν
τὸ τῆς δικαιοσύνης, διὰ τὸ φαίνεσθαι πολὺ τὸ πρὸς
τὸν λόγον ἀσύγκλωστον· καίτοι κἀνταῦθα τοῖς
καρποῖς χρῆσθαι εἰώθαμεν, οὐ μὴν σὺν τοῖς καρποῖς κατακόπτειν καὶ τὰ πρέμνα. τὸν δὲ σιτικὸν
καρπὸν καὶ τὸν τῶν χεδρόπων αὐανθέντα καὶ εἰς
γῆν πίπτοντα καὶ τεθνηκότα συλλέγομεν, ζῴων δὲ
τὰ θνησείδια [πλὴν τῶν ἰχθύων, ἃ καὶ αὐτὰ βίᾳ
ἀναιροῦμεν] οὐκ ἄν τις προσενέγκαιτο· ὥστε πολὺ
τὸ ἄδικον ἐν τούτοις. . . . οὕτως τὰς μὲν εἰς φυτὰ
βλάβας καὶ <διὰ> πυρὸς καὶ ναμάτων ἀναλώσεις
κουράς τε προβάτων καὶ γάλα βοῶν τε ἐξημέρωσιν καὶ κατάζευξιν ἐπὶ σωτηρίᾳ καὶ διαμονῇ τοῖς

true that if all creatures had an abundance of food, they would not behave aggressively toward one another or toward humans. For it is food, as necessary and simple as that is—and territory—that is the source of both their enmities and their alliances. Now if *humans* were hemmed into as tight a spot as animals on this score, they would become more aggressive than even the animals with reputations for aggression. Indeed, both war and famine have shown it, in which cases humans don't stop short of eating *one another.* And yet even without the conditions of war and famine people still eat tame, domesticated animals. . . .

Our concept of justice does not, however, extend to plants, for plants are clearly incompatible with *logos.* Yet even here it is our custom to make use of the *fruits*, not to chop the tree down at the trunk, fruit and all. Moreover, we gather wheat and legumes when they are dried out and falling to the ground, already dead, whereas no one would eat a dead animal, except a fish—and yet we destroy those, too, through violence. There is, then, a great injustice in these matters. . . . Contrariwise, to harm plants, to use fire and spring water,[25] to shear and milk sheep, and to yoke oxen—God grants forbearance to those who do

χρωμένοις ὁ θεὸς δίδωσι συγγνώμην, ζῷα δὲ ὑπά-
γειν σφαγαῖς καὶ μαγειρεύειν ἀναπιμπλαμένους
φόνου, μὴ τροφῆς ἢ πληρώσεως χάριν, ἀλλ᾽ ἡδονῆς καὶ λαιμαργίας ποιουμένους τέλος, ὑπερφυῶς
ὡς ἄνομον καὶ δεινόν.

. . .

20. . . . τῇ χρείᾳ τὸ πρὸς ἡμᾶς ὁρίζοντες οὐκ ἂν
φθάνοιμεν ἑαυτοὺς ἕνεκα τῶν ὀλεθριωτάτων
ζῴων, οἷα κροκόδειλοι καὶ φάλαιναι καὶ δράκο-
ντες, γεγονέναι συγχωροῦντες. ἡμῖν μὲν γὰρ
οὐθὲν ἀπ᾽ ἐκείνων ὑπάρχει τὸ παράπαν ὠφελεῖ-
σθαι· τὰ δὲ ἁρπάζοντα καὶ διαφθείροντα τοὺς πα-
ραπίπτοντας ἀνθρώπους βορᾷ χρῆται, μηδὲν ἡμῶν
κατὰ τοῦτο δρῶντα χαλεπώτερον, πλὴν ὅτι τὰ μὲν
ἔνδεια καὶ λιμὸς ἐπὶ ταύτην ἄγει τὴν ἀδικίαν, ἡμεῖς
δὲ ὕβρει καὶ τρυφῆς ἕνεκα παίζοντες πολλάκις ἐν
θεάτροις καὶ κυνηγεσίοις τὰ πλεῖστα τῶν ζῴων φο-
νεύομεν. ἐξ ὧν δὴ καὶ τὸ μὲν φονικὸν καὶ θηριῶ-
δες ἡμῶν ἐπερρώσθη καὶ τὸ πρὸς οἶκτον ἀπαθές,
τοῦ δ᾽ ἡμέρου τὸ πλεῖστον ἀπήμβλυναν οἱ πρῶτοι
τοῦτο τολμήσαντες. οἱ δὲ Πυθαγόρειοι τὴν πρὸς τὰ
θηρία πραότητα μελέτην ἐποιήσαντο τοῦ φιλαν-
θρώπου καὶ φιλοικτίρμονος.

. . .

these things for maintenance and survival. But to subject animals to slaughter and to butcher them, thus infecting oneself with murder, not for the sake of food or a full belly, but with pleasure and gluttony as its objective, that is utterly unlawful and terrible. . . .

Moreover, if we define what falls in our purview as need, we'd have to be quick to concede that we ourselves have come to exist for the benefit of the deadliest animals like crocodiles, whales, and snakes, which provide absolutely no benefit for us, but snatch and destroy any humans that cross their paths and use them as food. In behaving so, they are doing nothing worse than we do, except that it is neediness and hunger that drive them to this injustice, whereas we murder most animals out of hybris and for the sake of luxury and often for sport in the amphitheaters and in hunting. Indeed, owing to these activities, that part of us that is murderous and beastly and insensitive to compassion is bolstered, and the people who first dared to engage in this behavior blunted the edge of our gentleness. Accordingly, the Pythagoreans made kindness to animals a form of training in humanity and compassion. . . .

26. ... νῦν δὲ πολὺ τὸ ἄδικον ποιοῦμεν ἀναιροῦν-
τες μὲν καὶ τὰ ἥμερα [ὅτι] καὶ τὰ ἄγρια [καὶ τὰ
ἄδικα], ἐσθίοντες δὲ τὰ ἥμερα· κατ᾿ ἄμφω γὰρ ἄδι-
κοι, ὅτι ἥμερα ὄντα ἀναιροῦμεν καὶ ὅτι ταῦτα θοι-
νώμεθα, καὶ ψιλῶς ὁ τούτων θάνατος εἰς τὴν βορὰν
ἔχει τὴν ἀναφοράν. προσθείη δ᾿ ἄν τις τούτοις καὶ
τὰ τοιαῦτα. ὁ γὰρ λέγων ὅτι ὁ παρεκτείνων τὸ δίκαιον ἄχρι τῶν ζῴων φθείρει τὸ δίκαιον, ἀγνοεῖ ὡς
αὐτὸς οὐ τὴν δικαιοσύνην διασῴζει, ἀλλ᾿ ἡδονὴν
ἐπαύξει, ἥ ἐστι δικαιοσύνη πολέμιον. ἡδονῆς γοῦν
οὔσης τέλους, δείκνυται δικαιοσύνη ἀναιρουμένη.
ἐπεὶ ὅτι τὸ δίκαιον συναύξεται διὰ τῆς ἀποχῆς τίνι
οὐ δῆλον; ὁ γὰρ ἀπεχόμενος παντὸς ἐμψύχου, κἂν
μὴ τῶν συμβαλλόντων αὐτῷ εἰς κοινωνίαν, πολλῷ
μᾶλλονπρὸς τὸ ὁμογενὲς τῆς βλάβης ἀφέξεται. ...
οὐ γὰρ δὴ μὴ μετὰ κακώσεως ἑτέρου τὴν ἑαυτῶν
σωτηρίαν ἀμήχανον ἡμῖν ὁ θεὸς ἐποίησεν· ἐπεὶ
οὕτω γε τὴν φύσιν ἡμῖν ἀρχὴν ἀδικίας προσετί-
θει· ... αὕτη μὲν γὰρ φιλανθρωπία τις ἂν εἴη, ἡ δὲ
δικαιοσύνη ἐν τῷ ἀφεκτικῷ καὶ ἀβλαβεῖ κεῖται παντὸς ὅτου οὖν τοῦ μὴ βλάπτοντος. καὶ οὕτως γε
νοεῖται ὁ δίκαιος, οὐκ ἐκείνως· ὡς διατείνειν τὴν
δικαιοσύνην καὶ ἄχρι τῶν ἐμψύχων κειμένην ἐν τῷ
ἀβλαβεῖ.

But as things are, we commit much injustice, first by killing both tame animals and aggressive and unjust animals, then by eating the tame ones. We are, I repeat, unjust on both counts: because we slaughter them, tame though they are, and because we feast on them, and their deaths have reference only for food. We could add to these arguments the following: Someone who says that to extend justice to animals debases it is unaware that he's not preserving justice at all, but increasing pleasure, which is inimical to justice. In any event, whenever pleasure is the goal, one sees justice in the process of being destroyed. To whom is it not clear that justice is increased by abstinence? The person who abstains from every animate creature, even those that do not strike a social compact with him, will all the more refrain from harm to his fellow kind. . . . For God did not make our own salvation impossible to achieve without wronging something else. If *that* were the case, he would have given us a nature that was the origin of injustice. . . . But justice lies in the principle of abstaining and of harmlessness toward everything that does no harm itself. This is how a just person thinks, not the other way,

27. . . . ἀλλ' εἰ πάντες, φασί, τούτοις πεισθεῖεν τοῖς λόγοις, τί ἡμῖν ἔσται; ἢ δῆλον ὡς εὐδαιμονή-σομεν, ἀδικίας μὲν ἐξορισθείσης ἀπ' ἀνθρώπων, δικαιοσύνης δὲ πολιτευομένης καὶ παρ' ἡμῖν, καθάπερ καὶ ἐν οὐρανῷ. . . .

namely, to extend a justice that consists in harmlessness to animate creatures, too.

But people might say, "If everyone were persuaded by these arguments, what will it mean for us?" Clearly, we shall be happy! Injustice will have been banished from the human realm, and justice will live among us as a fellow citizen, as it does in heaven.

NOTES

Acknowledgments

1. Part of the European Union's Horizon 2020 research and innovation program, grant agreement No. 945408.

Introduction

1. Jenny Diski, *What I Don't Know about Animals* (New Haven, CT: Yale University Press, 2011); Temple Grandin, *Animals Make Us Human: Creating the Best Life for Animals*, with Catherine Johnson (Boston: Mariner Books, 2010); Donna J. Haraway, *When Species Meet* (Minneapolis: University of Minnesota Press, 2007); Christine Korsgaard, *Fellow Creatures: Our Obligations to the Other Animals* (Oxford: Oxford University Press, 2020); Vicki Hearne, *Animal Happiness* (New York: HarperCollins, 1994).

2. Vicki Hearne, *Adam's Task: Calling Animals by Name* (New York: Knopf, 1986), 68, italics in the original.

3. The possibilities of a relational approach to human-animal interaction are on full display in the mesmerizing film *Winged Migration* (BAC Films, 2001), where directors Jacques Perrin, Jacques Cluzaud, and Michel Debats imprint themselves as the mothers of newly hatched geese, storks, and pelicans, whom they teach to follow them in camera-quipped aerial paragliders and ultralights along the birds' routes of seasonal migration.
4. See James C. Scott, *Against the Grain: A Deep History of the Earliest States* (New Haven, CT: Yale University Press, 2017), 37–67.
5. Nastassja Martin, *In the Eye of the Wild*, translated by Sophie R. Lewis (New York: New York Review Books, 2021). Treadwell's love for the grizzlies of Alaska's Katmai National Park, too, despite his mental instability and naiveté (as captured on reels and reels of home video edited by Herzog), is nonetheless touching and profound.

1. Small Is Beautiful

1. Heraclitus of Ephesus (ca. 535–ca. 475 BCE) was a cryptic, paradoxical thinker, and possibly, too, a guru-like personality. In this anecdote we are meant to imagine visitors coming from afar to consult him as if he were an oracle and being sur-

prised to find the great sage huddled up and warming himself by a humble bread oven in the kitchen. Since Heraclitus taught that fire, owing to its dynamic, changeable nature, was the primary substance of which the universe is composed, the saying "there are gods here, too" refers to the idea that the fire in the oven partakes of the great cosmic fire that governs the universe, which for all intents and purposes, since it is the world's creative life force, is divine. Aristotle relies on his readers' knowledge of all this to suggest the same is true of humble, even ugly animals—that they have the same value for study as any other creature because they form part of the larger whole of Nature.

3. MY OCTOPUS TEACHER

1. These mere few lines involve several clever double entendres that are impossible to capture adequately in translation. The word *ēthos*, for example, translated as "cast of mind," originally meant the habitual "haunt" or "den" of an animal, only later to be used to describe human behavior. The word *orgē*, rendered as "mood" and "attitude," refers primarily to natural inclination or instinct, but it, too, was extended to denote human emotions and dispositions. *Poluplokos* ("complex"),

the adjective Theognis applies to the octopus, evokes the many *poly-* epithets attached to the wily hero Odysseus in Homer. And finally, *prosomileō*, meaning "cling to" here, also means "converse with" and "associate with" (as one would do with friends).

4. The Quality of Mercy

1. In the translation I have omitted several—but not all—occurrences of the repeated word *inquit* ("he says"), which is sprinkled throughout the passage to indicate (or suggest) Gellius's direct quotation of Apion's account.

5. Escape Artists

1. Sphinxes and satyrs: primates of some kind, perhaps gibbons or baboons, so named after their perceived resemblance to these mythological creatures.
2. That is, the termite.
3. Aelian simply calls it "the sailor" (*nautilos*). The name "Argonaut"—referring to the myth of Jason and his crew, the Argonauts (= "sailors of the ship Argo")—is still the commonly used descriptor for this octopod species today.
4. Beaver meat was prized by hunters for its fishy taste, but it is actually the musky oil (*castoreum*,

from *castor*, "beaver") located in its internal castor sacs (not testicles—both male and female beavers have castor sacs) that they are after, which was used for a variety of medicinal purposes in antiquity and as a food additive. Some folk etymology seems to lurk behind this lore given the phonetic similarity of *castor* to *castro* ("castrate"), but in fact the two words are not related.

6. ANIMAL SPIRITS

1. For an analysis of this letter's stylistic fireworks, see my commentary in *A Student's Seneca: Ten Letters and Selections from "De Providentia" and "De Vita Beata"* (Norman: University of Oklahoma Press, 2006). For a discussion of its ecological significance in the context of Stoicism, see my *Plato's Pigs and Other Ruminations: Ancient Guides to Living with Nature* (Cambridge: Cambridge University Press, 2020), 147–50.

2. Seneca means that parents often pray for their children to enjoy material wealth or high social status, the acquisition of which can interfere with the pursuit of ethical, philosophical lifestyles.

3. "Accursed prayers" translates *execrationes*, which can mean both negative curses and positive prayers.

4. Sallust (86–35 BCE), a historian, was the Roman Thucydides. This quotation comes from the preamble to his *Conspiracy of Cataline* (1.1–2).

7. LIONS, AND TIGERS, AND BEARS

1. A territory corresponding to the modern Balkans region.
2. Perhaps an exaggerated description of large wild mountain sheep or goats, or aurochs, once common in Europe, now extinct. I have seen donkeys spray liquid feces quite some distance in self-defense when agitated, so that is not an implausible detail.
3. The Geloni were a Hellenized subset of the nomadic steppe peoples of Eurasia known as Scythians. The location implied here corresponds roughly to modern Ukraine.
4. This moose-like creature seems to be legendary and makes its way from the description here via Pliny and Aelian all the way through the Middles Ages to Rabelais. But some mammals do indeed change the color of their fur according to the seasons in northern climes: the stoat, for example, and the arctic fox.
5. A region in northwestern Turkey.
6. Bears foam at the mouth under duress. Camels spit. The European polecat sends forth putrid

spray that would make anything inedible. Verdict: some mishmash of animal behaviors seems to inform this description.

7. This seems merely to describe the physiological effects of fear felt by prey when stumbling upon a predator. I felt it once when turning a corner in the Black Hills of South Dakota with two small children in tow and meeting a bison face to face. On the special eeriness of hyenas, see Porphyry's remarks in selection no. 12.

8. Herodotus (*Histories* 2.68) reports this same detail, that the so-called *trochilus* bird picks leeches out of crocodiles' mouths in the Nile. So-called cleaning symbiosis does exist in Nature among birds and beasts, especially in marine and riverine environments, for instance, between the oxpecker and the rhino, though this specific interaction between the sandpiper and the crocodile has been observed only occasionally in the wild.

9. True! I have seen exactly this happen to a poor donkey in Italy.

10. This detail is derived from Aristotle's discussion of penises at *History of Animals* 9.6. The marten does happen to have an extensive *baculum* or penis bone, as any ancient hunter who had skinned one would have noticed. That its powdered form cures strangury is, of course, folkloric.

11. True, and readily verified by observation.

12. Thessaly is on the great migration path of many species of birds and serves as a breeding ground for storks even today. Their annual return and their feeding on snakes would have invited Thesssaly's ancient inhabitants to consider them sacred.

13. There is nothing important to disbelieve or falsify here. Mice come in many shapes and sizes.

14. Seriphus is a small Greek island in the Aegean. Male frogs croak most vigorously in spring because there is moisture to breed.

15. The flesh of animals that feed on plants toxic to humans and other animals can itself be poisonous—quail, for example, that feed on hemlock causing coturnism.

16. It seems likely the observer has mistaken the sinuous contests between rival *male* adders in courting a female for the mating ritual itself. For the former, see this remarkable video filmed at Kariega Game Reserve in South Africa: www.kariega.co .za/blog/is-this-a-puff-adder-mating-ritual. As for the mother's young bursting through her belly, unlike most snakes, adders do not lay eggs, but give live birth to as many as twenty offspring at parturition.

17. Laurence Totelin's explanation at "The Recipes Project" (recipes.hypotheses.org/1898) of why seal's rennet might have been thought to be

helpful in treating epilepsy is as fascinating as it is convincing.

8. Quoth the Raven Nevermore

1. Stesichorus was a Greek lyric poet from Sicily (ca. 632–552 BCE). The story of the nightingale alighting on his lips at birth is recounted in the *Palatine Anthology* = Testimonium no. 44 in David A. Campbell's *Greek Lyric* (Loeb Classical Library 476).
2. The ancients uniformly thought female birds were the virtuoso singers, whereas in most species it is actually the male.
3. The ring-necked parakeet is meant. The manuscripts add the short phrase that the bird is called *siptaces* in the Indian vernacular, which is probably a copyist's mistake for *psittacus*, "parrot."
4. "Generals" translates *imperatores*, which could mean the bird's trainers, or, just possibly, "emperors."
5. That is, Nero, Agrippina's son, and Britannicus, Claudius's son, both by previous marriages. (Nero later had Britannicus poisoned.)
6. Drusus was Tiberius's brother, Germanicus Drusus's son.
7. This is where Hannibal retreated (*rediit*) from his assault on Rome, hence the deity "Rediculus,"

whose shrine on the Appian Way memorialized that event.

8. Scipio died in 129 BCE, believed by some to have been assassinated by political opponents at Rome. He led the Roman forces that defeated and sacked Carthage in 146 BCE and Numantia in 133 BCE.

9. The year was 35 or 36 CE, a year before Tiberius's own death.

9. PATHETIC FALLACY

1. The god of the bow and lyre is Apollo.
2. A town on the Cycladic island of Ceos.
3. Ovid's language suggests the stag has been tricked out to resemble a statue.
4. "Amulet" here in Latin is *bulla*, a pendant worn by Roman boys that proclaimed their status as freeborn children and served to ward off malevolent spirits. Ovid's inclusion of this detail adds to the pathos of the story (the amulet fails to protect the stag) and suggests that Cyparissus is, tragically, anthropomorphizing his pet.
5. Meaning that the sun is directly overhead.
6. Apollo.
7. Cyparissus, in case it's not obvious, has been transformed into a tree.
8. In antiquity, as today, the cypress was a tree typically planted in cemeteries.

10. The Elephant in the Room

1. Pliny's nephew, the younger Pliny, in a letter to the historian Tacitus (6.16), pays tribute to his uncle and reconstructs the circumstances of his death. Both he and Suetonius highlight the elder Pliny's eagerness to observe the volcano's eruption out of scientific interest. Some modern scholars have suggested rather that Pliny's main purpose, since he was commander of the fleet at nearby Misenum, was to rescue stranded survivors. Whatever his primary motive, it certainly wouldn't be the only time a naturalist or scientist has died in the pursuit of knowledge. Dian Fossey, Marie Curie, David Douglas, Aldo Leopold, and Khaled al-Asaad, and, recently, Dom Phillips and Bruno Pereira, provide a few well-known examples.

2. These attributes make the elephant an ideal Roman citizen—perhaps especially in its obedience to authority (*imperium*) and its mindful discharging of duties (*officia*).

3. Mauretania was the Roman name for the Maghreb, an area of North Africa sandwiched between the Atlas Mountains to the south and the Mediterranean coast to the north, extending westward as far as the Atlantic Ocean. In Roman times, it comprised roughly the territory of the modern states of Algeria, Tunisia, and Morocco.

NOTES

4. The idea seems to be that the elephants make their handlers swear such an oath (*iusiurandum*) before setting off to sea, knowing that they—the handlers—would be bound by religion to honor it.

5. Father Liber is Dionysus/Bacchus, one of whose mythological exploits was to have conquered the East with his rites and returned with an entourage of celebrants in triumph. Pompey's triumph commemorated his military victory over the rebel forces of Gnaeus Domitius Ahenobarbus in North Africa in 81 BCE.

6. A Pyrrhic dance was an ancient Greek war dance characterized by quick, darting movements imitative of feints on the battlefield. A close analog perhaps familiar to some is the Maori *haka* dance performed by the New Zealand All Blacks rugby club.

7. Gaius Licinius Mucianus had been suffect (replacement) consul during the reigns of Nero, then Vespasian. He wrote a memoir, now lost, containing observations about the geography and natural history of the Roman East, based on time spent on a military campaign in Armenia and the Levant and as governor of Syria.

8. Herodotus, *Histories* 3.97. Juba II (ca. 48 BCE–23 CE) was the client king of Roman Numidia and Mauretania. As a boy he was brought to Rome as war booty by Julius Caesar, educated in Greek

and Latin, and became one of the most learned men of the day. He fought alongside Octavian (Augustus) at the Battle of Actium against Cleopatra and Marc Antony.

9. Polybius (ca. 200–ca. 118 BCE), detained at Rome as a hostage during Rome's conquest of Greece, wrote a history in Greek of Rome's rise to power in the second and third centuries BCE. The passage Pliny refers to here is *Histories* 39.1.2. Gulusa was the son of Numidian king Massinissa (ca. 238–148 BCE), whom Polybius claims to have met.

10. I have inserted this paragraph here from a later section of book 8 (10.31).

11. Lucius Coelius Antipater, a Roman jurist and historian, contemporary of Gaius Gracchus (ca. 154–121 BCE), whose works are lost.

12. That is, the *Origines*, a lost historical work in seven books by Cato the Elder (234–149 BCE).

13. Aristophanes of Byzantium (ca. 257–180 BCE) was a noted Homeric scholar and director of the Library at Alexandria.

14. Bocchus (ca. 110–ca. 80 BCE) was client king of Roman Maurentania.

15. The verb used suggests condemnation to death by fighting in the arena.

16. Pompey was beheaded by Caesar's henchmen on the shores of Egypt while trying to escape after his defeat at the Battle of Pharsalus (48 BCE).

11. Pigs Is Equal

1. As it has come down to us, the treatise seems to be incomplete.
2. Plutarch plunges in *in medias res*, assuming the reader's knowledge that, in Homer, Circe has just given Odysseus instructions before his departure from her island on how to descend to the Underworld, where he must consult Tiresias for further information about his journey home to Ithaca (*Odyssey* 10.483–540).
3. Circe had previously tried to turn Odysseus into a pig, too, only Athena sent Hermes to give the hero the miraculous protection of a plant called *moly* (*Odyssey* 10.274–322).
4. According to the timelines of the *Iliad* and the *Odyssey*, twenty years have elapsed since Odysseus set sail from Ithaca for Troy, suggesting that his wife, Penelope, is at least in her forties.
5. Hecate was the patron goddess of witches like Circe.
6. This phrase is a parody of a well-worn Homeric greeting formula (compare, for example, *Odyssey* 10.325) except that the verb is in the past tense.
7. Gryllus is referring obliquely here to his own change from human to animal.

8. Another typical Homeric form of address (the Cephallenians were a people over whom Odysseus ruled), just possibly with a sarcastic pun on the Greek word *kephalē*, "head," thus "king of Brainiacs."

9. Gryllus uses the plural, which indicates his criticisms are directed not only *ad hominem*, but *ad homines*.

10. Described at *Odyssey* 9.108–11.

11. Characterized thus at *Odyssey* 13.242–47.

12. An echo of the description of the Cyclops's land at *Odyssey* 9.109.

13. "Sacker of cities" (*ptoliporthos*) is an epithet used of Odysseus at *Iliad* 2.278. "Fierce" (*thrasus*) is a common way to describe heroes in both Homeric poems.

14. "Unflinching" translates *schetlios*, another common epithet for heroes in Homer, which can mean "stalwart," but more often means unflinching in cruelty or disregard, i.e., "merciless."

15. Two recurring epithets for Odysseus in Homer speak volumes about his tricks and machinations: *polymētis* ("wily") and *polymēchanos* ("resourceful"). It was he, for example, who came up with the idea of the Trojan Horse (*Odyssey* 8.499–520) and blinded the Cyclops Polyphemus by treachery (*Odyssey* 9.252–479).

16. A vivid description of an animal's death throes if ever there was one.

17. "Cowardice" in Greek is literally "unmanliness" (*anandreia*), so conveys some irony here.

18. An attempt at etymological wordplay with *douleuein* ("serve as a slave to") and *deilia* ("timidity").

19. The manuscripts here read *parrhēsia* ("frankness in speech"), a hallmark of Cynic virtue, but that seems out of context here. One scholar suggested an emendation to *eutharseia* ("fierceness"), and some such word seems more in keeping. I have split the difference in translation with "boldness."

20. Theseus's slaying of this animal is recounted by Plutarch in his *Life of Theseus* sec. 9, where he gives the rationalizing interpretation that the sow, named Phaea, was really a female bandit nicknamed the Sow "because of her life and manners." Crommyon was a Greek village located between Megara and Corinth.

21. For the many ancient references to the Sphinx at Thebes, whom Oedipus vanquished and whose riddle he solved, see J. G. Frazer's note in Apollodorus (*The Library* 3.5.8) (Loeb Classical Library 121).

22. The fox was a scourge sent by Dionysus to ravage the Thebans. See Pausanias, *Description of Greece*

NOTES

9.19.1. The phrase "mischievous monster" seems to be a quotation from a lost work.

23. The snake is the Pythoness, who protected the Oracle when Earth controlled it, before the advent of Apollo. See, for example, Ovid, *Metamorphoses* 1.438–62.

24. Echepolos ("Horse-keeper") by name. See *Iliad* 23.295–97.

25. Penelope employed the ruse that she would marry again only after she had finished weaving a burial shroud for her father-in-law, which she unraveled every night, to keep the suitors at bay (*Odyssey* 2.93–110 = 19.137–56). Penelope was the daughter of Icarius, a brother of Tyndareus, and so a first cousin of Helen of Sparta. Spartan women, like Spartan men, were renowned for their bravery and fierceness.

26. That is, women as renowned for daintiness as Spartan women were for toughness, to whom Penelope might also be compared.

27. Plutarch engages briefly here in the ancient debate over whether humans are what we are by nature or by nurture, or, in Greek, *phusis* versus *nomos*.

28. "Wolf-minded" is a hero's proper name at *Iliad* 15.430; for "lionhearted," see *Iliad* 6.639, 7.228, and, predicated of Odysseus himself, *Odyssey* 4.724; for "like a boar in strength," see *Iliad* 4.253.

29. "Spirit" translates *thumos*, a word from the earliest times, possibly for the organ in the body, located in the chest, that animates it—"heart," perhaps. (One scholar has proposed that the *thumos* is the diaphragm, or the lungs.) In any event, the *thumos* is the seat of the emotions, and the word came to be used to designate that among philosophers. Plato's "spirited element" of the tripartite soul, for example, resides in the *thumos*.

30. The Greeks mixed their wine with water before drinking.

31. That is, the spirit/*thumos*.

32. In fact, Odysseus did sleep with Circe (*Odyssey* 10.336–47), instructed to do so by Hermes (10.297) as a stratagem to secure the transformation and safe release of his men. Perhaps one can give Plutarch the benefit of the doubt that, as Homer depicts it, he did so reluctantly. Or perhaps this is a clue that we are not to take Gryllus's sophistry too seriously.

33. In discussing the Egyptian equivalent of the libidinous, goat-like god Pan, Herodotus notes that he had heard a contemporary story suggesting the opposite, that an Egyptian woman did in fact have ritual intercourse with a billy goat in the region of Mendes (*Histories* 2.46).

34. Compare Aelian, *The Peculiar Behavior of Animals* 3.9.

35. There appears to a lacuna in the text here.

36. "Fancies," here and elsewhere, translates the word *doxa*, which carries philosophical connotations of "mere opinion" or "illusion." Plato, for example (cf. *Republic* 479d–e), distinguishes strongly between *doxa* and true knowledge (*epistēmē*).

37. Plutarch is referring obliquely to luxury items imported from abroad.

38. A compressed continuation of the metaphor highlighting the moral pitfalls of living in a port city.

39. Phrygia and Caria were regions in Anatolia (modern Turkey) where coinage was invented and thus proverbially renowned for their wealth. Dolon was a Trojan warrior paid off by Hector to spy on the Greeks but slain by Odysseus and Diomedes (as recounted in *Iliad* book 10). Priam was the king of Troy.

40. Compare Herodotus, *Histories* 2.84.

41. Probably a reference to birds.

42. Folkloric inferences perhaps rooted somehow in observation of animal behavior.

12. ABSTINENCE MAKES THE HEART GROW FONDER

1. Castricius, a Roman senator, was a fellow member with Porphyry of a group that studied with the philosopher Plotinus (ca. 205–70 CE), whose

Enneads, a work that Porphyry compiled and edited after Plotinus's death, formed the basis for Neoplatonism. Castricius, Porphyry tells us earlier in this treatise, had abandoned a vegetarian diet, and Porphyry's task at hand is to attempt to reconvert him.

2. "Abstinence" translates *apochē*. By abstinence Porphyry means specifically refraining from killing and eating animals, but also restraint of desires and impulses more generally.

3. An allusion to Plato, *Philebus* 67D, where the animals in question are horses and cattle. Porphyry's substitution of pigs and goats suggests special lasciviousness.

4. Pythagoreans, like Buddhists and Hindus, believed in the reincarnation of human souls into other life forms, so were vegetarians on that account. Porphyry himself does not believe in reincarnation but invokes Pythagoras here because he was, along with Empedocles, the standard-bearer for a vegetarian diet among Greek philosophers.

5. *Logos*, a Stoic technical term, means both "language/speech" and "rational thought/reason" and captures in a single word how the two interact. Because Porphyry's argument in the opening paragraphs depends on this complex association of rationality and language, for the time being I leave the word untranslated. Where language per se is

less at issue I translate *logos* and its derivatives with words like "rational," "reason," and "rationality."

6. The Stoics were insistent that wisdom sets its bar high. As Seneca puts it in *De vita beata* (17.3), "I am not a sage . . . nor shall I ever be. . . . Don't demand of me that I be on par with the best, only that I be better than the bad. It is enough for me to minimize my faults each day and correct my mistakes."

7. "Self-interest" is *philautia* (lit. "love of self") and has negative connotations. It's not perfectly clear what Porphyry means. Is he saying that the Stoics are engaging in speciesism? Or are they making an elaborate philosophical excuse just to continue eating meat?

8. The Greek words *phōnē* and *glōtta*, translated here as "sound" and "tongue," can also mean "voice" and "language" respectively. The verb translated as "speak" (*phtheggetai*) can also mean simply "utter sounds." In the *Politics* (1253a10–18) Aristotle says that animals have only *phōnē*, which they use to express pleasure and displeasure, whereas humans possess *logos*, whose function and purpose is to distinguish right from wrong. The Stoics, whom Porphyry is criticizing here, followed Aristotle on this point.

9. Porphyry neglects to say here that humans are perfectly capable of learning languages not their

own. He assumes monolingualism for the sake of the argument, as his focus here is on what linguists would call phonetics, not phonemics. Further below he shows he is aware of human multilingualism.

10. Apollonius of Tyana was an itinerant Pythagorean holy man who was active in the time of Nero. The story is recounted in Philostratus's *Life of Apollonius of Tyana* (4.3), where the bird is a sparrow and an enslaved boy, not a donkey, is what trips and spills the grain. The point of the story in Philostratus is that this mishap provides a bonanza meal for the birds and that the sparrow is showing generosity in sharing the good news with his fellows. Melampus and Tiresias are soothsayers and diviners from Greek mythology who possessed the ability to talk to animals. (For Melampus, see Apollodorus, *The Library* 1.9.11; for Tiresias, 3.6.7.)

11. This, according to Apollodorus (note previous), is how Melampus acquired his ability to understand animal speech.

12. Marcus Licinius Crassus (115–53 BCE) was a Roman general and statesman, famously the richest man at Rome. This story, with small variations, is told also by Plutarch (*On the Cleverness of Animals* 976a) and Aelian (*The Peculiar Behaviors of Animals* 8.4), who adds the detail that Crassus's

eel had been adorned with earrings and small necklaces set with jewels, "just like some lovely maiden."

13. "Capacity to formulate a mental image" translates *phantasia*, a notoriously difficult technical term in ancient Greek philosophy.

14. From the next sentence, it's clear that Porphyry means their greediness to *eat* them.

15. "Experience" that is natural and "disease" that is not are both expressed in Greek by the word *pathos*. Porphyry focuses on our shared morbidity first and will address shared *pathē* of perception in the next paragraph.

16. That is, internal *logos*.

17. That is, go mad.

18. Obviously, one of several instances of folkloric belief reported in this treatise.

19. The Greek syntax and thought of this sentence are rather compressed and elliptical, though the sense is not in doubt. I've done my best to clarify.

20. "Morbidity" = negative *pathos*.

21. Lynceus ("Lynx-eyed"), a Greek hero from the earliest times, is said to have had x-ray vision such that he could see things buried underground (Apollodorus, *The Library* 3.10.3).

22. Porphyry quotes a snippet here, almost shorthand, from a larger passage from Homer (*Iliad* 17.673–78) where Menelaus, on the rampage to help avenge

Patroclus's death, is compared to an eagle. The fittingness of the larger passage reveals the degree to which Porphyry (or his source) has internalized his voluminous reading. Here is the translation by A. T. Murray, as revised by William Wyatt (Loeb Classical Library 121): "So saying, tawny-haired Menelaus went away, glancing warily on every side like an eagle, which, men say, has the keenest sight of all winged things under heaven, by whom, though he be on high, the swift-footed hare is not unseen as he crouches beneath a leafy bush, but the eagle swoops on him and swiftly seizes him, and takes away his life."

23. The translator can verify the utter truth of this statement from experience.

24. Stork offspring were observed to take care of their parents, providing both food and shelter for them, whence the origin of "Stork Laws" in antiquity that required citizens to take care of their parents in old age. (See D'Arcy Thompson, *A Glossary of Greek Birds* [Oxford: Clarendon, 1895], 128.)

25. It is unclear how the use of fire and water from streams would be an exception to the rule of "do no harm." Porphyry might be referring to the use of fire to burn over scrub pastures to stimulate growth and to diverting water from streams for irrigation (which could adversely affect the flora and fauna in riverine ecosystems).

RESOURCES AND PASSAGES
TRANSLATED

Resources

In addition to the books cited in the introduction, the reader may find the following scholarly and reference works helpful.

Arnott, W. Geoffrey. *Birds in the Ancient World from A to Z*. New York: Routledge, 2017.

Campbell, Gordon Lindsay. *The Oxford Handbook of Animals in Classical Thought and Life*. Oxford: Oxford University Press, 2014.

Fögen, Thorsten, and Edmund Thomas, eds. *Interactions between Animals and Humans in Graeco-Roman Antiquity*. Berlin: De Gruyter, 2017.

Kitchell, Kenneth. *Animals in the Ancient World from A to Z*. New York: Routledge, 2013.

Passages Translated

Selection 1 from Aristotle. *Parts of Animals. Movement of Animals. Progression of Animals.* Translated by A. L. Peck and E. S. Forster. Loeb Classical Library 323. Cambridge, MA: Harvard University Press, 1937.

Selection 2 from Babrius and Phaedrus. *Fables.* Translated by Ben Edwin Perry. Loeb Classical Library 436. Cambridge, MA: Harvard University Press, 1965.

Selection 3 from Tyrtaeus, Solon, Theognis, and Mimnermus. *Greek Elegiac Poetry: From the Seventh to the Fifth Centuries BC.* Edited and translated by Douglas E. Gerber. Loeb Classical Library 258. Cambridge, MA: Harvard University Press, 1999.

Selection 4 from Gellius. *Attic Nights.* Vol. 1, *Books 1–5.* Translated by J. C. Rolfe. Loeb Classical Library 195. Cambridge, MA: Harvard University Press, 1927.

Selection 5 from Aelian. *On Animals.* Translated by A. F. Scholfield. Vol. 1, *Books 1–5.* Loeb Classical Library 446; vol. 2, *Books 6–11,* Loeb Classical Library 448; vol. 3, *Books 12–17,* Loeb

Classical Library 449. Cambridge, MA: Harvard University Press, 1958, 1959, 1959.

Selection 6 from Seneca. *Epistles*. Vol. 1, *Epistles 1–65*. Translated by Richard M. Gummere. Loeb Classical Library 75. Cambridge, MA: Harvard University Press, 1917.

Selection 7 from Aristotle. *Minor Works: On Colours. On Things Heard. Physiognomics. On Plants. On Marvellous Things Heard. Mechanical Problems. On Indivisible Lines. The Situations and Names of Winds. On Melissus, Xenophanes, Gorgias.* Translated by W. S. Hett. Loeb Classical Library 307. Cambridge, MA: Harvard University Press, 1936.

Selection 8 from Pliny. *Natural History*. Vol. 3, *Books 8–11*. Translated by H. Rackham. Loeb Classical Library 353. Cambridge, MA: Harvard University Press, 1940.

Selection 9 from Ovid. *Metamorphoses*. Vol. 2, *Books 9–15*. Translated by Frank Justus Miller. Revised by G. P. Goold. Loeb Classical Library 43. Cambridge, MA: Harvard University Press, 1916.

Selection 10 from Pliny. *Natural History*. Vol. 3, *Books 8–11*. Translated by H. Rackham.

Loeb Classical Library 353. Cambridge, MA: Harvard University Press, 1940.

Selection 11 from Plutarch. *Moralia*. Vol. 12, *Concerning the Face Which Appears in the Orb of the Moon. On the Principle of Cold. Whether Fire or Water Is More Useful. Whether Land or Sea Animals Are Cleverer. Beasts Are Rational. On the Eating of Flesh*. Translated by Harold Cherniss and W. C. Helmbold. Loeb Classical Library 406. Cambridge, MA: Harvard University Press, 1957.

Selection 12 from Porphyre. *De l'abstinence*. Introduction by Jean Bouffartigue and Michel Patillon. Compiled and translated by Jean Bouffartigue. Vol. 3. Paris: Les Belles Lettres, 1977–95.